Strong, Slim, and 30!

Eat Right, Stay Young, Feel Great, and Look Fabulous

LISA DRAYER, M.A., RD

New York Chicago San Francisco Lisbon London Madrid Mexico City
Milan New Delhi San Juan Seoul Singapore Sydney Toronto

The **McGraw·Hill** Companies

Library of Congress Cataloging-in-Publication Data

Drayer, Lisa.
    Strong, slim, and 30! / by Lisa Drayer.
        p.   cm.
    ISBN 0-07-146497-2 (alk. paper)
      1. Women—Nutrition.   2. Women—Health and hygiene.   3. Reducing diets.
  I. Title.   II. Title: Strong, slim, and thirty!

  RA778.D836   2007
  613.2′5—dc22   2006022867

The recipe for Chilled Banana Latte in Part 2 is used with permission of the Mid-Atlantic Dairy Association.

1 2 3 4 5 6 7 8 9 10 11 12 13 14 15 FGR/FGR 0 9 8 7 6

ISBN-13: 978-0-07-146497-0
ISBN-10:   0-07-146497-2

Interior design by Think Design Group, LLC

McGraw-Hill books are available at special quantity discounts to use as premiums and sales promotions, or for use in corporate training programs. For more information, please write to the Director of Special Sales, Professional Publishing, McGraw-Hill, Two Penn Plaza, New York, NY 10121-2298. Or contact your local bookstore.

The information contained in this book is intended to provide helpful and informative material on the subject addressed. It is not intended to serve as a replacement for professional medical advice. Any use of the information in this book is at the reader's discretion. The author and publisher specifically disclaim any and all liability arising directly or indirectly from the use or application of any information contained in this book. A health care professional should be consulted regarding your specific situation.

This book is printed on acid-free paper.

To my wonderful parents,
Barbara and Barry Drayer.
Your unconditional love and support
made this book possible.
I love you.

Contents

Foreword

Here's what I know about young women today: They're smart, they're confident, and they know a whole lot more about who they are and where they're going than the world at large gives them credit for. They like to run hard, they love to eat, they enjoy a good sweat, and they really appreciate a dry martini (or two) on a Friday night after a long week at work. They like a good laugh. They don't have a lot of free time, and they don't have much faith in big government or big business. They do stress about finances and their careers, and whether that size 4 is still going to fit next year. They do yoga and they lift weights. They're ambitious, competitive, and strong—in every way. Their passion and drive can sometimes be intimidating. But they care deeply for their families, and they want a loving partner and kids in their world. They expect to live long, healthy lives, and when it comes to health and emotional well-being, they care a lot. They know they need to take care of themselves now, and they're willing to do that in order to live better lives later on.

All of which is precisely why Lisa Drayer's *Strong, Slim, and 30!: Eat Right, Stay Young, Feel Great, and Look Fabulous!* is so timely and so perfectly in step with today's generation of young women. Because Drayer herself recently hit the big 3-0, she has a firsthand, from-the-heart understanding of her 30-something readers—and a fresh voice and youthful perspective that make for a unique and even deeper connection. Drayer knows exactly what practical and emotional challenges her audience is up against because she faces them every day. She also knows that it's the physical signs of wear and tear that preoccupy her readers the most—those damn little fine lines around your eyes, that last handful of Oreos now sitting on your hips, and those jeans from college that you can't get into anymore.

To those in-your-face (and in-the-mirror), scary changes, Drayer offers up a whole new outlook on food and nutrition—what she calls "a real-life plan for long-term health and beauty." To her credit, she admits this is no quick fix. In fact, it's a whole lot better than that. *Strong, Slim, and 30!* is a science-based plan that will carry you through your 30s and well beyond. It's about losing weight without losing the important antiaging and bone-building nutrients that are vital to your diet. Sounds logical, right? Well, believe it or not, this diet *and* health plan is the very first of its kind. And let me tell you, it's about time!

It's also incredibly simple. Using all of the nutritional tips and secrets she's been sharing with her friends for years, Drayer provides a full guide to healthy eating—calorie-controlled options for breakfast, lunch, and dinner, and a one-of-a-kind roster of antiaging, bone-building, and comfort food snacks. It's a totally doable regimen that's adaptable to any lifestyle, whether you're toeing the line on your career or at home with the kids, and whether you feel empowered to take charge of your future or you're just trying to lose another five pounds before your *next* birthday.

The book is divided into three parts. In Part 1, Drayer deftly explains the science behind what's happening to your body, including how you can boost your metabolism, eat for beauty, and take a more mature, long-term approach to weight loss that will help you lose the pounds—and keep them off. Part 2 gives you the nuts and bolts of *Strong, Slim, and 30!* and features a range of calorie-controlled meal plans (from 1,200 to 1,600) that you can easily tap into depending on your individual goals and needs. Part 3 shows you how the plan applies to every part of your life—including preparing for pregnancy, dining out, hitting the town, and maintaining your health for the long term. Best of all, throughout the book, Drayer uses real-life stories from women who have been on the plan to show you the high points, the speed bumps, and the inevitable success of *Strong, Slim, and 30!*. And hey, there's no stronger endorsement than hearing from one of your peers that something actually works.

There are a lot of weight-loss plans and calorie-counting programs out there. And, believe me, as the editor in chief of *Women's Health*, I've seen 'em all. That's why this one stands out—it's smart, it's healthy, it's practical, and it's absolutely doable. Most of all, it carries the same promise for real, long-lasting success as today's generation of young women.

Kristina M. Johnson
Editor in Chief
Women's Health

Acknowledgments

I would like to express my sincere thanks to the many individuals who helped to make *Strong, Slim, and 30!* a reality.

To my agent, Stacey Glick: Thank you for making this project happen and for your terrific guidance and support every step of the way. I am grateful for our relationship. A special thank-you to Jessica Papin, for urging me to write a health book for women our age.

To my editor, John Aherne: Thank you for your wonderful insight and feedback and for being so attentive and supportive. I am thrilled that I had the opportunity to work with you. Special thanks to Julia Anderson Bauer, Lizz Aviles, Sarah Love, Amy Morse, Sarah Pelz, and Tom Lau: I am so lucky to have all of you on my team! A very special thank-you to the entire staff at McGraw-Hill, for its hard work, dedication, and enthusiasm for this project.

To my wonderful friend, and talented journalist, Jenette Restivo: Thank you for doing such a great job in writing the case studies and for all of your feedback and support throughout. To Jessica Fishman, M.S., R.D.: Thank you for all of your help in building terrific meal combinations to fit the 30s nutrient criteria. I can always trust you to do a fantastic job. To Lisa Young, Ph.D., R.D.: Thank you for reading over the entire manuscript and for offering invaluable feedback.

I am especially grateful for my terrific family at *Women's Health* magazine. Thank you, all, for being so enthusiastic and supportive of this project. Special thanks to my colleagues and friends from CNN and WCBS-TV. Carol Costello: Thanks for all of your support and enthusiasm. Dave Price: Thank you for all of your support and encouragement, especially during the final hours.

A special thank-you to Lori Ferme, for always being so helpful and supportive, and to Cyndi Fink, who was there from the beginning. I would like to express my sincere appreciation to plastic surgeon Dr. Aron Kressel, for welcoming me into his office. I am grateful to the American Dietetic Association for being an invaluable resource to me and my career. I am indebted to my nutrition professors at Cornell University and to the Science, Health, and Environmental Reporting Program at New York University.

I am especially grateful to my wonderful friends and family who are near and dear to my heart. Dr. Irving Buterman and Ellen Finkelstein: Thank you for all of your support in my career endeavors and for providing me with a wonderful office to counsel the success stories in this book. I am so lucky to have you both in my life. To Sherry Buonasera, a dear friend who will always be in my heart: You modeled strength, beauty, and compassion. I know you are celebrating this book with me.

My deepest love and appreciation to my mom and dad; my amazing brother, Jeff; my loving grandparents, Edie and Bernie Cooper and Sylvia and Nat Drayer; and Ali: I am so lucky to have you all in my life, and I cannot thank you enough for your love, support, and encouragement throughout every stage of my life.

Introduction

Before you learn about my plan for staying strong, slim, and sexy in your 30s and beyond, let me tell you a bit about me. As a nutritionist and health reporter, I spend a lot of time teaching individuals how to eat to stay young and healthy. Still, while many people think I meet my "nine-a-day" quota of fruits and vegetables, always say "no" to desserts, and hit the gym five days a week, the reality is my lifestyle is far from this type of perfection. In fact, I am conscious of my weight, I have a big sweet tooth, and I struggle with getting to the gym. (Oh, and I rarely have time to cook during the week.) On top of all that, I've hit the big 3-0. You know what that means: more responsibilities, more challenges, and more health changes going on. A pound or two (or three or four) here, gray hairs over there, lines on your face that you swear weren't there a week ago. Sound familiar? If so, you have plenty of company. The good news is that there are things you can do to maximize your health and beauty, and I'm here to share with you all I've learned. Despite my less-than-perfect lifestyle, I have managed to keep my weight down and look my best by eating an antiaging diet that still includes sweets (and by taking jazz-funk classes). So, get ready to learn how to become a more fit, fabulous, glowing you!

Reaching the Big 3-0

Welcome to the 30s club! By now, you probably have acquired valuable knowledge about who you are and what you want in life. After all, this is the decade immediately following the soul-searching 20s, when you made your first decision about which path your life would take. Nevertheless, my guess is that you're a bit confused—not just about general life stuff that continues to come your way, but also about one of the most important subjects of all: how to best take care of your body and your health. As career responsibilities and personal relationships consume more time and energy at this stage of your life, maintaining a healthy lifestyle and a svelte figure becomes more and more challenging.

I don't have to tell you that your body is signaling the age change. You feel it in your sluggish metabolism—or your inability to eat half a box of Mallomars and stay at your current weight on the bathroom scale. You're aware of all those not-so-sexy changes going on—no longer can you eat a bag of potato chips for hold-me-over snacks and scarf down pizza slices for dinner while still fitting into those slender Levi's. Nor can you go for handfuls of jelly beans or licorice ad libitum without gaining a single pound—even if it's a temporary pound. Perhaps you have tried shedding 5, 10, maybe 15 pounds several times but can't seem to find the formula that will *keep* the weight off. Or maybe you're not sure which foods give you the best energy and simply allow you to look your best.

You might have recently given birth to the most precious little baby, and the pounds you gained during pregnancy just don't seem to come off as quickly as you would like. Maybe you're thinking about a new addition to your family, but you want to drop 10 pounds first and quickly begin an eat-healthy insurance diet. Perhaps you're worried about being able to shed 5 pounds in time for your one, two, or five-year wedding anniversary, when your husband is planning an escape that requires packing your slim and sexy lingerie.

Maybe this is the first time you're struggling with weight loss, or it's just become noticeably harder, and you're afraid that given your chaotic lifestyle, your slim figure will slip by as fast as your 29th year did! Speaking of your 30th birthday, you probably realized that the hype associated with leaving your 20s behind was blown out of proportion. Looking back, you now see that there was really nothing to fear. In fact, the 30s may have brought along a sense of clarity that the 20s could never offer.

Many Happy Returns

I want you to know that the same applies to your health. With the right advice, you can adopt a much clearer, more mature outlook on your health—an outlook with longevity and staying power. It's no longer about doing a crash workout to look good in your bikini for the weekend at the beach. It's about a healthy, happy, more mature you, whose beauty has staying power. And don't fret: you can absolutely achieve slimness, even during this busy time. Take it from someone who is always searching for answers and solutions in this health-conscious yet hectic world. I'm going to tell you how to stay strong, slim, and sexy—now and for the rest of your life. Get ready for a real-life nutrition plan to keep you looking and feeling your best throughout your exciting years ahead.

PART 1

The Science of *Strong, Slim, and 30!*

The 30s Health Prescription

A Real-Life Plan for Long-Term Health and Beauty

As someone whose job involves covering the latest nutrition news, I know that every week there seems to be another new diet—another "Lose 10 pounds in two weeks" fix; another slimming plan for staying youthful, beautiful, and glamorous forever. It's no wonder we're confused as to what the best eating plan would entail. The options are endless and enticing at the same time. And while we may have considered trying the latest bestseller, we still refuse to give up our bagels, pizza, ice cream, chocolate, french fries, and other foods we've come to know and love. That state of affairs leads me to break my own nutrition news, which is that it's probably time to change your diet, even while keeping all the other balls in the air that you happen to be juggling. In fact, the 30s are the ideal time to make this lifelong investment. By adopting a diet that incorporates balanced nutrition within your own individualized calorie budget, you can have lifelong health, beauty, strength, and slimness!

My idea for this book was to give every female who is approaching 30 or who is in her 30s and beyond a unique, reliable, and practical antiaging nutrition plan to incorpo-rate in her day-to-day life. I was frustrated seeing friends and clients trying to lose weight by following many of the gimmicky fad diet books that line bookshelves everywhere. Maybe they had lost 5 pounds after the first week on the diet, and maybe they even continued to lose here and there, but for all of them, it was impossible to maintain that weight loss over the long term. Whether I was helping a working woman or a stay-at-home mom, each expressed similar nutritional needs and concerns that the diet books failed to address satisfactorily.

Inside this book are all of the nutritional secrets I've been sharing for years with friends and colleagues in their late 20s, 30s, and beyond. So, count yourself in as a member of the club. Here you will learn the best eating plan for your specific physical, emotional, and lifestyle needs. I'm going to arm you with healthy tactics to lose weight, enhance your nutritional well-being, and defy the effects of age on your body.

Enter "The 30s Health Prescription"

The 30s Health Prescription is *the* diet plan designed for you—a busy, hip, 30-something woman desiring a sensible nutri-tion road map to keep you healthy, slim, and sexy. It's a plan that you can count on for guidance when you're in a diet dilemma and need some sound, girlfriend nutrition advice. If you don't know what to dish up for dinner, or if a calorie reality check is overdue; if you want information on the best foods to eat for beautiful skin and hair or nutritional tips to fight disease; if you just want some tips on what to order at your favorite restaurant or some advice on how to best shed those pregnancy pounds—The 30s Health Prescription will be there for you! Plus, it's guaranteed to make you feel great, inside and out. Best of all, this is no passing trend. It's a new outlook on food and nutrition. You are going to be so diet savvy after reading this book that you won't need me, or any other health professional, to tell you what you should and shouldn't eat. You will know how to identify meal combinations that will help you keep a slim figure, while incorporating important snacks to keep you youthful and thoroughly satisfied. Before you know it, you'll be leading the rush to Bloomingdale's bikini department rather than pulling out last year's swimsuit!

A Peek at Your Plan

Achieving a healthy body may seem more difficult than it was when you were a sweet, young 20-something. Most likely, there are some new priorities for you other than your body. You may be at a pivotal point in your career, taking your relationship to a new level, even considering starting a family. You may have children already. Whatever your life situation may be, those biweekly body-sculpting classes take a backseat to many other obligations. The 30s is a time when you are essentially overwhelmed by monumental, life-changing decisions, coupled with day-to-day stress. Staying slim may not be at the top of your must-do list—or, if it is, accomplishing the task may seem nearly impossible. Whether you consider yourself fortunate in this respect or not, I want you to know that you *don't* have to stress over what you are going to eat for your next meal.

Don't get me wrong: adopting a new approach to eating is no simple task. It won't necessarily happen overnight. But it doesn't have to be overwhelming. Deciding what to eat for your 3 P.M. snack when you're about to snooze at your computer keyboard doesn't have to be complicated. So, the first thing I'm going to tell you is that my plan is *simple*: I offer you calorie-controlled options for breakfast, lunch, and dinner, and a list of antiaging foods ("A"), bone-building foods ("B"), and comfort foods ("C") as snacks.

Your breakfasts will be high in fiber and will include foods rich in antioxidants and bone-building nutrients. Fiber is extremely beneficial for weight loss and can help protect against age-related diseases, too. Fruits such as strawberries, raspberries, and blueberries contain antioxidants and other vitamins that are essential for optimal health. Calcium-rich foods such as yogurt, low-fat milk, and even fortified cereals are important for preserving your bone mass as you age, and getting enough of the mineral helps to ward off osteoporosis.

Your lunches and dinners will include calorie-controlled meal options, balanced with protein, vegetables, and whole grains. The best part is that you can choose what you want to eat: you can have home-cooked meals or frozen dinners if you wish, as long as they fall within your calorie allotment and meet the 30s criteria of being moderate in protein and low in fat, particularly the harmful kind. Here's a quick snapshot of The 30s Health Prescription:

1. Choose an antiaging breakfast that is rich in calcium, antioxidants, whole grains, and fiber.
2. Picture your lunch and dinner plates in thirds: one-third protein, one-third vegetables, one-third grains.
3. Add your "ABC's"—your antiaging ("A"), bone-building ("B"), and comfort foods ("C")—as snacks.

If this doesn't sound simple, don't worry. All of your meals and snacks have been designed to conform to the nutritional guidelines I've mentioned, so you don't have to think about it much. And remember, you don't have to worry about calorie calculations either—they're done for you!

By following The 30s Health Prescription, you will lose weight, but you will also keep your body healthy at the same time. Calories are important, but so are antiaging and bone-building nutrients. Looking and feeling good on a Saturday night counts, but you want to look good for lots of Saturday nights!

In addition to the health aspects of this stage in your life, my plan takes into account real-life events and offers solutions to your unique issues. You will find tricks that worked for many of your peers, including how to balance a healthy diet with a hectic life, how to make pregnancy pounds disappear, and how to stay slim when enjoying nights out. In other words, unlike many strict low-carb regimes, diet pills, and other weight-loss fads, your 30s plan is not a quick fix; it's a long-term program for good health and happiness, for now and for your future!

A Peek at What Happens in Your 30s

It's an unfortunate fact that your metabolism slows down in your 30s. Your peak bone mass is achieved. Wrinkles and fine lines start to appear. You may experience high cholesterol for the first time or a slight increase in blood pressure. Fertility issues may be a concern now. Because of these not-so-pretty facts of nature, you need a whole-body solution for staying strong and slim.

Truth be told, I'm going through the same changes you are. There are days when I feel as if I can eat just one cookie and it "sits on me." Then there's the calcium issue: as is the case with 90 percent of women our age, I can't say that I get the daily recommended amount from food. Then there is the feat of juggling it all—while trying to avoid stress-eating and being careful to not go overboard at restaurants, parties, holidays, and other fun events. And of course, I'm constantly searching for the best foods for optimal energy.

So, I'm going to share with you a plan I designed specifically to suit *our* needs. It's a diet that will keep you happy, healthy, and looking your best at all times, just as it has done for so many women. Following my plan doesn't mean you won't be able to fit into that new pair of jeans you've been dying to wear in just a few weeks. You *will* see short-term results come your way. But more important, with my plan, you will have the body you want forever. This is the plan to make you strong, slim, and sexy, in your 30s and for many, many years beyond!

Lauren's Story

When I first met Lauren, my 30-something friend, she told me that her typical diet had been a blueberry muffin or a bagel with cream cheese for breakfast; Chinese food for lunch, and pizza for dinner. Having three or four beers after work, skipping exercise, and paying no attention to what she ate had often accompanied her late-20s lifestyle.

Lauren was aware that her prior eating habits were not necessarily going to help her drop the 20 pounds she was looking to lose, but she didn't know how to go about changing what had to be changed—especially because she had tried lots of diets without great success throughout her 20s.

Lauren emphasized that sticking to strict rules as she'd previously tried to do wasn't an option anymore, because while she wanted to be at a healthy weight, she also wanted to enjoy her life. And that life had become much more hectic: she changed careers, she had a demanding and time-crunched job, and she recently started living with her boyfriend. She didn't have the time or patience at this point to count fat grams or worry about carbs.

When I asked Lauren what her top two diet downfalls were, she cited some food issues that are pretty universal among our age-group. The first was the "all-or-nothing" syndrome— thinking that if you're going to eat healthy, you have to eat healthy all of the time. This style of thinking led Lauren to binge when she fell off track. The second main diet downfall for Lauren was nighttime eating—nibbling on empty calories throughout the evening, or even downing half a bag of tortilla chips and salsa for dinner, especially when she came home late. Lauren simply didn't know what she should eat for dinner, and many times, dinner took the form of a snacking binge.

The first goal I worked on with Lauren was to change her perspective on eating and challenge her thinking on what constituted the "perfect" diet. I informed her that a nutritious weight-loss plan can include small indulgences, even on a daily basis, and would prevent feelings of deprivation. So, right off, we worked on incorporating a "sweet budget" in Lauren's plan, with a specific allotment of 100 calories per day. (If she exercised on a particular day, we boosted the sweet budget up to 200 calories.) In this way, a healthy diet was one that included sweets. From a psychological point of view, this feature worked extremely well for Lauren.

I also believed that Lauren would benefit from having simple rules when it came to deciding what to eat, especially for lunches and dinners. I worked with Lauren on the "30s plate": one-third protein, one-third carbohydrates (ideally whole grains), and one-third vegetables. As I reviewed Lauren's list of favorite foods, I came up with meal combinations that fit The 30s Health Prescription formula.

After a couple of weeks, Lauren told me that the 30s plate approach was working out well for her. The lunch and dinner meal ideas proved simple enough to follow, and she liked the fact that the guidelines I gave her didn't require much thought.

Lauren continued to struggle with what to eat for snacks, but I listened carefully when she told me that some snacks had become dietary staples and were in her diet to stay! I came up with different snack ideas for each "A" (antiaging), "B" (bone-building), and "C" (comfort foods) category, making a point to include Lauren's favorite snacks: chips and salsa, Oreos, and low-fat cheese.

Lauren loved the fact that she could have a comfort snack each day. She found that being able to have this treat made The 30s Health Prescription livable and doable. Putting all of her diet pieces together, Lauren quickly shed the weight she'd been hoping to lose—22 pounds! But Lauren told me that the most rewarding part of the diet was the fact that the guilt she previously associated with dieting was nonexistent on The 30s Health Prescription. She discovered that by using simple guidelines for her meals, and by eating her favorite snack foods in controlled portions, she could enjoy her life and still lose weight—a concept she had heard before but never really understood. And weight in Lauren's 30s was a bigger matter than just size 10 jeans; heart disease and diabetes run in her family, and by eating nutritionally balanced meals and snacks, she was optimizing her chances of combating these diseases. What's more, Lauren found that the lifestyle approach to her eating carried over into her exercise habits. She had started training for her first 5K, and The 30s Health Prescription gave her a needed energy boost for her weekly runs.

Lauren is just one of many success stories of The 30s Health Prescription. You too can achieve the slimness, strength, and good health that Lauren and others have attained on this fabulous eating plan!

Boosting Your Metabolism

(2)

The 30s Health Prescription for Staying Slim

I received the following e-mail message from a woman named Erica, in Forest Hills, New York: "I am 33 years old and have been dieting for the last 15 years. I have tried everything from Jenny Craig to Weight Watchers to all of the latest diet fads. I want to learn how to eat the right combinations of food for my body and enhance my sluggish metabolism. Can you help me learn how to incorporate good eating habits into my lifestyle—and keep the weight off for good?"

As I read those words, it occurred to me how common Erica's story was. Over the years, during conversations with clients as well as friends, more women than I can count have been frustrated by the same set of circumstances: a sluggish metabolism like never before coupled with futile efforts at shedding pounds. So, I can tell you that if you identify with Erica, what you are experiencing is totally normal, and many 30-somethings are eager to sympathize with you.

The next point I want to convey is that you don't have to be burdened by a slow metabolism. There are ways to boost it, and that's what I'm psyched to share with you. Get ready to learn how to achieve the best calorie-burning potential possible.

No More Cookies, Candy, and Chips— Without Pounds Attached

One of the most glaring changes that we 30-something women will face together is a calorie-burn slowdown. Our ability to consume large portions of the fattening, sugary, or salty goodies we love without gaining any weight inevitably comes to a halt. We can no longer eat those Oreos, Doritos, M&Ms—you name it—and not gain a pound or two or three. On top of that, trying to *lose* weight may seem harder than ever before.

A case in point is the rude awakening of my stick-thin cousin Brett. Brett *loved* snacking on Mallomars. I think those yummy chocolate-covered marshmallow graham cookies served as regular meals for her. Amazing as it sounds, up until her late 20s, she could eat a box of Mallomars in one sitting and not gain a single pound. I would watch dumbstruck and ask myself: *how* does she manage to have regular cookie binges and maintain a size 2?

Brett continued to devour Mallomars to her heart's content and look fabulous in bikinis and tight jeans—until one day, when her amazing calorie-burning potential came to a halt. She was visiting at my parents' house that summer and decided to weigh herself on the bathroom scale. At the time, she was in her early 30s. When she stepped on the scale, she was astonished at the number she saw. She had gained five pounds within a month.

Welcome to a new era of a sluggish metabolism. The hard reality is that, on average, your metabolism will decline by about 3 percent to 4 percent during your 30s and each decade after. Translation: about four to six pounds gained per year, if you don't compensate through diet and physical activity.

Metabolism Meltdown

Why the slowdown? One reason is hormones. Danielle Day, Ph.D., Research Physiologist in the Military Nutrition Division at the U.S. Army Research Institute of Environmental Medicine and an expert on female metabolism, explains that at around age 25, we experience declines in growth hormone and dehydroepiandrosterone (DHEA). These two hormones perform central roles in preserving muscle mass, and the more muscle we have, the greater our metabolism, because muscle burns more calories than fat (more on this ahead). Then, of course, huge lifestyle changes are taking place too. In our early 30s, we're busy with our careers (maybe sitting at a desk most of the day, to boot) and perhaps starting families, and chances are that we have less time for the gym. Skipping workouts greatly contributes to our inability to keep eating what we used to eat with no repercussions.

The upside is that there's a lot you can do to make sure your metabolism is running at full speed, keeping your body in top shape. And in case you're wondering if you have to totally give up Oreos, Doritos, and M&Ms—the answer is no. This book is not about deprivation. Rather, the plan takes into account your desire for sweet and salty snacks, while keeping portions in check.

In fact, a big part of the plan is based on the nature of metabolism. For that reason, it's helpful at this point to make sure we've got the terminology and other details straight. Metabolism is the energy produced (think calories burned) from all of the chemical reactions taking place in the body. Resting metabolism is what the body burns at rest, when performing its daily routine activities such as breathing, pumping blood, and regulating body temperature. (Note: resting metabolic rate, or RMR, is commonly interchanged with basal metabolic rate, or BMR; however, RMR is slightly higher.) Resting metabolism accounts for up to 75 percent of your total energy expenditure, or calories burned each day.

According to a study published in the *Journal of Nutrition*, the brain and organs including the heart, liver, and kidneys total only about 5 percent of body weight, but they account for 70 percent to 80 percent of resting metabolism, due to their high activity levels (think of this as "organ metabolism"). Muscle mass, on the other hand, constitutes about 35 percent of body weight but accounts for only about 20 percent of resting metabolism. Your "fat-free mass" includes both of these

Metabolism for Thought

In addition to biological factors such as body weight and muscle mass, our metabolism is influenced by specific body states. For example, metabolism increases during periods of rapid growth, such as pregnancy, when our bodies are making new cells. Additionally, when you have a fever, your body temperature increases, and this also increases your resting metabolism. Other medical conditions, including cancer and severe burns, increase metabolism. Increased or decreased levels of thyroid hormones can increase or decrease resting metabolism, a condition that can be orrected with medication. Even extreme weather—such as very hot or very cold temperatures— can increase your resting metabolism.

components—internal organs and skeletal muscle mass. The study found that an age-related decline in resting metabolism is attributed to a decrease in fat-free mass, but there is no evidence for a decline in organ metabolism in healthy adults. Thus, changes in metabolism with age—especially around our 30s and up—are attributable to a decrease in muscle mass with age. In fact, starting in our 30s, women tend to lose about one-quarter to one-half of a pound of muscle mass each year, while gaining up to one pound of fat.

Our resting metabolism is also correlated with other biological factors, one of which is weight. The more you weigh, the higher your metabolism, and when you lose weight, your metabolism declines, because a smaller body burns fewer calories. In addition to body weight, metabolism is based on factors such as age (as you can see, for the reasons revealed in the study, the older you are, the fewer calories you burn), height (the taller you are, the more you burn), general activity level (the more you move around, the more you burn), and gender (ladies, unfortunately, burn fewer calories than men, because we have less muscle mass).

The reason I focus so much on resting metabolism is that it's responsible for more than two-thirds of your total energy expenditure. Other contributors to the total amount of energy you expend include calories burned from exercise or physical activity (about 15 percent to 30 percent of total energy expenditure, depending on activity level) and calories burned from digesting, absorbing, and metabolizing the nutrients in the food you eat—known as the thermic effect of food (also known as diet-induced thermogenesis). The thermic effect of food is associated with a slight increase in body temperature. It comprises a small amount of energy expenditure—roughly 10 percent of the total amount of calories consumed—though it can range from 6 percent to 15 percent, according to Carla Wolper, M.S., R.D., clinical coordinator of the Obesity Research Center at St. Luke's–Roosevelt Hospital, in New York. The thermic effect of food is affected by the composition of your diet and is greater for large meals and meals that are high in protein.

Age, Gender, and Weight Explained

Let's recap: The reason your metabolism slows in your 30s is that as you age, you lose muscle mass (which accounts for about 20 percent of your resting metabolism) and gain more body fat. While fat in your body is needed to insulate and protect your organs, fat also burns fewer calories than muscle. So, with a higher percentage of body fat, you ultimately burn fewer total calories. Moreover, women, by nature, have a higher percentage of body fat than men—and thus tend to burn fewer calories. Now add to this the fact that *as you lose weight—and fit into smaller-sized clothes—your metabolism naturally decreases*. Remember, a smaller body burns fewer calories, and it requires even fewer to continue shedding pounds.

Here's a quick example. Suppose I weigh 150 pounds, and I consume (and burn) 2,300 calories each day to maintain that weight. If I start consuming only 1,800 calories each day, I could lose about 1 pound a week, because I'm burning 500 more calories than I'm consuming (500 calories/day × 7 days per week = 3,500 calories, which translates to 1 pound). But once I get to a weight of, say, 135, I am no longer burning 2,300 calories, because my resting metabolism is lower, as a result of my smaller body size. In fact, at a weight of 135, I may be burning 2,100 calories. If I continue to consume those 1,800 calories, my daily excess calorie burn would now be 300 instead of 500. Over a week, I would lose *less* than 1 pound—unless I cut back my intake to 1,600 calories, which would result in a daily excess burn of 500 calories again. So, as you can see, the less I weigh, the fewer calories I burn—and the fewer calories I can consume if I want to keep losing weight. Simply put, you need to periodically cut back on your calories as you lose weight, in order to keep shedding pounds.

Burn, Baby, Burn!

Despite an inevitable slowdown, 30-year-old women like you and me can keep that metabolism churning at full throttle and thereby keep our bodies in beautiful shape. And here's the icing on the cake: considering this is the decade in which you start to experience a drop, it's also an opportunity to nip the problem in the bud. So, time to stop fretting and give the old metabolism a serious boost. I'm going to arm you with practical, simple steps to rev up your internal engine and keep your body in top calorie-burning mode. Before you know it, you'll be reveling in your efforts, while getting closer and closer to fitting into that pair of Sevens you've been longing to wear. And no stress, either—the tips I'm about to discuss are already incorporated in your 30s meal plan (Chapters 5 through 8).

Small, Frequent Meals

It's hard to believe, but it's a fact: eating burns calories. When you eat, your body expends energy digesting and absorbing nutrients in foods. This thermic effect of food, as noted earlier, is equivalent to about 10 percent of your daily calorie intake.

You may have heard that eating small, frequent meals is one of the keys to losing weight, but you may not have known why, until now. The simple reason is that when you eat small meals throughout the day, your body must continuously burn calories as it digests, absorbs, and metabolizes the food.

Think about it: when your body is breaking down carbohydrates, proteins, and fats into smaller nutrients that get absorbed in the bloodstream, it's busy "at work." The net result of all of this internal activity is that you are burning calories, even though you probably don't feel as if you are exerting much effort at all. Because of the calorie-burning benefits associated with eating small, frequent meals, The 30s Health Prescription calls for three meals and three snacks a day, which can be eaten three to four hours apart.

Skipping Meals = Sluggish Metabolism

When you skip meals, or stagger meals too far apart, your body senses what's going on. It recognizes that it's not getting fed, and so it conserves energy instead of burning it. Your metabolic engine compensates by slowing down to a less-than-optimal speed. The end result is that you burn fewer calories. In fact, skipping meals and consuming far fewer calories than what is considered healthy can lower resting metabolism by as much as 20 percent. That means up to 400 fewer calories are burned each day. By contrast, when you feed your body small, frequent meals, you are constantly fueling it, enabling it to function optimally and burn more calories.

In case this all sounds too good to be true, I offer some research findings to support my case. One recent study published in the *American Journal of Epidemiology* revealed that individuals who ate four or more meals each day had a lower risk of weight gain compared with those who consumed three or fewer meals. Additionally, skipping breakfast was associated with increased prevalence of obesity in the study group.

Granted, the amount you burn from digesting and absorbing food isn't huge. I mean, you can't skip your cardio workouts. It comprises only 10 percent of total calories, but that's enough to make a difference, as shown by the journal study. What this means for us 30-something women is that we need to eat small meals and snacks, every three to four hours, to get full calorie-burning benefits.

And here's a bonus that should not be overlooked: eating more often makes you less likely to be famished at mealtime and, therefore, less likely to overeat.

Protein Power

Another important factor in keeping your metabolism running at full speed is including an adequate amount of protein in each meal, which helps to preserve muscle mass. Retaining muscle is key, because muscle burns more calories than body fat. The more muscle you have, the more calories you burn. The not-so-great news here is that in addition to the age factor, you lose some muscle as you lose weight. Approximately 25 percent of every pound lost is muscle tissue. What this means is that if you don't include enough protein in your diet to offset body losses, you will suffer a drop in metabolism directly related to a loss of muscle during weight loss.

A recent study published in the *Journal of Nutrition* underscored protein's power in helping individuals lose weight. Women who consumed more protein lost more body fat and less muscle mass, compared with those who ate less protein but the same number of calories. Researchers theorize that protein-rich foods offer us a dose of leucine, an amino acid that helps to preserve muscle mass and metabolism.

There are other pluses to protein. This nutrient, which is found in animal- and plant-based foods, has a satiating effect. Consuming a meal with protein makes us feel fuller and can help us to consume fewer calories overall than a meal that consists only of carbohydrates and fat. Also, compared with carbohydrates, it's more difficult for the body to metabolize protein, so you expend lots of energy (and burn calories) digesting it. This helps to explain the greater thermic effect of protein.

PROTEIN VERSUS FAT. A recent study from the University of Washington School of Medicine and the Oregon Health and Science University illustrates the extent to which protein helps to suppress your appetite. In the study, 19 participants followed three types of diets: a weight-maintaining diet for two weeks consisting of 15 percent protein, 35 percent fat, and 50 percent carbohydrate; then a diet with the same calories but consisting of 30 percent protein, 20 percent fat, and 50 percent carbohydrate for two weeks; after the first four weeks, the participants were allowed to consume as many calories as they liked, as long as they followed the diet that consisted of 30 percent protein.

The study participants re-ported feeling less hungry on the higher-protein diet, even though the total calories during the first four weeks were the same. What's more, when they were allowed to eat as much food as they liked on the higher-protein plan, *their intake decreased by 441 calories per day, and they lost an average of 11 pounds, including 8 pounds of fat*!

YOUR PROTEIN PRESCRIPTION. On this plan, your days include 20 percent to 30 percent of total calories in the form of protein, which will help you lose weight and preserve muscle mass at the same time. Aim for *at least* three ounces of protein per meal—for a quick visual guide, the size of a computer mouse or a deck of cards. Your "B" snacks will boost your protein intake as well.

Susan's Story

Susan, a mother of two and an at-home baker of wedding cakes and other fancy desserts, came in to see me for weight loss. She wanted desperately to lose 20 pounds and was having great difficulty. What frustrated Susan the most was that, whereas she had always been able to burn off the cake crumbs and chocolate chips she nibbled on while baking, the times had changed. Now chocolate chips translated to pounds on the hips, even when she controlled her portions.

I took a look at Susan's food diary and noticed that she was eating three meals a day, about five to seven hours apart. She would have breakfast at around 8 A.M., lunch usually at around 1 P.M., and dinner at around 8 P.M. Susan typically baked in the late afternoon, at around 3 or 4 P.M. At this point, she was usually hungry but would hold off from eating until dinner. Hence her cravings for cake crumbs.

I immediately realized that Susan would benefit from eating small, frequent meals—adding one between breakfast and lunch, and another between lunch and dinner. Her spacing of meals was too stretched out, and this was slowing her metabolism and contributing to her late-afternoon cravings. In addition, she frequently ate starchy foods that were low in protein, such as frozen lasagnas and other pasta meals.

Along with downsizing her portions, I taught Susan to divide her plate into thirds (equal servings of protein, vegetables, and grains), to ensure that she was getting enough protein. The protein would help her to feel full and reduce cravings. Because Susan often ate frozen dinners for lunch, I advised her to look for ones that contained at least 20 grams of protein, and to add some chicken strips or a slice of turkey to ones that contained less.

We also built "A," "B," and "C" snacks into Susan's meal plan, and we limited her

Yo-Yo Dieting

You may have been told that yo-yo dieting—a cycle of losing weight and then regaining it—is associated with a decreased metabolic rate. A study from the University of Pennsylvania sheds some light on the assumed relationship. The study examined the dieting behaviors of 50 obese women and found no evidence to suggest that yo-yo dieting (also known as "weight cycling") is associated with a decreased resting metabolism or an increased percentage of body fat.

While the study may provide some optimism for yo-yo dieters, it shouldn't be taken out of perspective. Losing and then regaining weight over and over can be mentally taxing and, from a psychological perspective, can make it harder to lose weight each successive time.

The overriding benefit of following The 30s Health Prescription is that the plan will keep you satisfied and slim for the rest of your life. On my plan, you lose the weight and *keep it off*.

comfort foods to 150 calories. One priority was making sure Susan always had some snacks with her, because she was frequently on the go, carpooling for her kids and doing other various errands. I suggested individually wrapped, calorie-controlled, calcium-fortified energy bars and soy chips for her to keep in the car, which would allow her to meet her "B" snack requirement. We also included a glass of skim milk or a low-fat yogurt as a midmorning bone-building snack before lunch and after her training session. Susan soon experienced greater energy, and fewer cravings for sweets when she baked. (When she does nibble, she counts it as her "comfort food" for the day.) Susan effortlessly lost 20 pounds in 15 weeks and is currently maintaining her new weight. She is also enjoying fabulous beach vacations in her favorite Caribbean spots.

In addition to cutting back on her portions, a key to Susan's weight loss was spreading her meals out. This meant there was more time in the day during which she was burning calories. Susan was constantly feeding her metabolic "engine," enabling it to avoid any slowdowns and function at full speed. By eating small, frequent meals and including a minimum of three ounces of protein with each one, Susan also experienced fewer cravings, the biggest saboteur of her diet.

Weights for Your Weight

In conjunction with eating small, frequent meals and getting enough protein, one of the best ways to boost muscle mass and metabolism is to gradually start lifting weights. An exercise program that includes just 20 minutes of weight training twice a week will help you preserve muscle during weight loss. Remember, you lose some muscle with every pound you shed. However, you can retain more muscle, and therefore burn more calories, when you tone your body by lifting weights. Simply by restricting calories and lightly ton-ing, you will keep your metabolism running optimally during your weight loss—even when you're not at the gym. Even if you have a job that requires you to sit all day, the more muscle you have, the more calories you burn!

Cardiovascular Exercise

The beauty of cardiovascular exercise is that it not only increases the amount of calories that are burned, but it also keeps metabolism at a higher rate for some time after you stop exercising. What's more, when you combine exercise with a decreased calorie intake, you lose mostly fat, versus solely restricting calories to very low levels (as low as 800 calories per day), which results in a loss of about 50 percent fat and 50 percent lean mass for each pound lost.

Sustaining cardiovascular exercise as you age is especially important. One recent study indicates that even when you cut back on calories to compensate for reduced activity, you may experience a slower metabolism as you age. In other words, if you don't take time to get out and walk for at least 30 minutes on most days, metabolism can shift into low gear, despite a corresponding decrease in calories. Aim to do some brisk walking (ideally 30 minutes per day) to jumpstart your metabolism and burn calories.

Now, Isn't That NEAT

Part of your total daily energy expenditure is derived from your day-to-day level of activity. I'm not talking about formal exercise, even though that's important, but rather your general, overall activity level—specifically, how much you move around. For example, if you have a job that requires you to be on your feet all day, you're going to burn more calories than you would if you had a desk job. Similarly, when you're cleaning your house or apartment, you're burning more energy than you are when sitting on the couch watching TV. All of this translates to something known as NEAT—non-exercise activity thermogenesis.

As defined in a Mayo Clinic study, NEAT encompasses the energy expended for everything you do that is not sleeping, eating, or sportslike exercise. Examples include walking, typing, performing yard work, and fidgeting. The study established that even trivial physical activities increase metabolic rate substantially, and it is the cumulative impact of a multitude of actions that culminates in an individual's daily NEAT.

A Metabolism Makeover

Here is a recap of my recommended strategies to make over your metabolism:

1. **Consume small, frequent meals.** Eat three meals and three snacks each day, spaced three to four hours apart. Never skip meals; keep portable snacks handy for times when you're too busy to stop and eat. Try to be consistent with meal and snack times.

2. **Include protein on your plate.** Aim to include *at least* three ounces of protein per meal. For proper portioning, visualize the size of a computer mouse or a deck of cards.

3. **Gradually start lifting weights.** Light weight lifting will help you to

What does this mean for you and me? We shouldn't underestimate the power of fidgeting, for one thing. In the study, obese individuals registered low NEAT and, on average, spent two and a half hours more in a chair each day than their slimmer counterparts—thus burning 350 fewer calories. If you have a job that requires you to sit all day, be sure to get up frequently, stretch, take walks, and use the stairs as often as possible. These small changes add up and can contribute to lots of calories burned. I think that's pretty neat!

preserve muscle mass, boost metabolism, and tone while you shed pounds.

4. **Start walking.** A brisk walk for at least 30 minutes each day will jump-start your metabolism and help you burn extra calories.

5. **Take advantage of all things NEAT.** I'm talking about fidgeting, stretching, walking up stairs, and even delivering messages in person instead of e-mailing whenever possible.

6. **Drink green tea.** This beverage may offer metabolism-boosting benefits!

Taking Time for Tea

Before we move on to more exciting ways to keep us strong, slim, and sexy, I have some beverage-related metabolism tips for you. First, let's chat about green tea.

Believe it or not, there's been lots of exciting research on green tea and its ability to fight fat. Green tea contains special chemicals known as catechins that may be helpful in boosting metabolism. One study from Switzerland found that individuals who consumed a combination of green tea extract and caffeine experienced a 4 percent increase in metabolism over a 24-hour period. (Those consuming caffeine by itself didn't experience any change in metabolic rate.) Researchers in Japan recently found that green tea extract helped to prevent excessive accumulation of body fat when fed to mice daily over several months. The beverage may also give a boost to your workouts: Another recent animal study found that green tea extracts (equivalent to four cups per day) improved endurance during exercise and increased the amount of fat burned during a workout.

While the research is preliminary, it provides some intriguing news about this beverage's ability to help us shed pounds.

Because tea is calorie free and can even help us feel calm and satisfied, I recommend consuming it whenever possible. If you are drinking lots of coffee (and adding half-and-half), it's probably time to take a tea break.

Weight Gain and PMS: The Metabolism Link

If you're like many other 30-somethings, you may be wondering: why does premenstrual syndrome cause me to gain weight? For an answer, we can turn again to Danielle Day, Ph.D., who says that lower levels of estrogen during one's period are related to an increased consumption of calories. Specifically, it's thought that estrogen levels affect energy peptides in the brain that stimulate us to eat. Here's how it works: When estrogen levels are low during the initial part of the menstrual cycle (when you're actually menstruating), levels of these peptides increase, and you tend to eat more than usual. Low levels of estrogen are also associated with a decrease in other peptides that normally tell you to *stop* eating. And, there's another piece contributing to weight gain: a decline in estrogen during this time (the early follicular phase) is directly associated with a lower resting metabolic rate. Day says when you measure RMR at different points in a 28-day menstrual cycle, you can see that metabolism is clearly decreased during the early follicular phase and then increases significantly in the midluteal phase (days 21 through 24), when both estrogen and progesterone are high. What this translates to is 30 fewer calories burned per day, over a 6-day period, or 180 fewer calories burned per cycle.

It's no wonder PMS is a prime time for weight gain! The problem is compounded if you're skipping workouts too, while eating more due to PMS cravings. To combat this PMS-induced weight gain, try cutting your "C" (comfort) snack in half. Or, burn an extra 30 calories during a workout. One thing, though: some of your weight gain will be related to water retention during PMS. Best advice: avoid the scale during this time of the month.

Weight Loss in a Bottle?

Many people are tempted to try to shed pounds with a little help from pills—so many, in fact, that it's a $40 billion industry and growing. Based on a report from the Center for Science in the Public Interest (CSPI), though, the only thing you'll lose with weight loss pills is your money. For example, CortiSlim is a dietary supplement that promises to make pounds melt away by suppressing cortisol, a hormone that increases in response to stress and has been linked to fat storage around the abdomen. But the CSPI said there's no good evidence to suggest that the supplement lowers cortisol levels, or even that doing so would promote weight loss. In fact, the report noted that the Federal Trade Commission charged the manufacturers with consumer fraud for claiming that CortiSlim results in rapid permanent weight loss of 10 to 50 pounds by lowering cortisol levels.

Conjugated linoleic acid (CLA), another supplement touted to help people lose body fat, is actually a mixture of fats that exist naturally in meat and dairy products. The most recent study has shown that CLA is effective in helping individuals lose weight—specifically about five pounds over one year. However, the long-term safety of CLA is unknown. Commenting on this point, the CSPI stated that the study raised some red flags with regard to inflammation and increased blood fats among those taking it.

While Trimspa (the ephedra-free version) was not cited in the report, it has certainly gained popularity in the world of weight-loss supplements. Trimspa contains many ingredients, including chromium, vanadium, and hoodia gordonii, which is an appetite suppressant derived from a South African plant. However, we don't know if hoodia is safe or if it works. I haven't yet seen any published evidence. Also, the full dose, which is six tablets per day, contains 300 milligrams of caffeine, which is what you get in three cups of coffee. So, you can expect stimulating effects as well.

There are other supplements that may speed up metabolism in the short term, such as guarana-containing supplements (guarana is an herb with high concentrations of caffeine) and other ephedra-like supplements. They come with undesirable side effects, however, including jitteriness and the potential for increases in blood pressure. In addition, high amounts of caffeine in supplements can cause blood sugar to drop, which can lead to intense cravings for sweets. Your best bet is to steer clear of these short-term, not-so-safe supplements and focus on safe, long-term weight loss.

Erica's Story: From Metabolism Mess to Success!

Erica, who was introduced at the beginning of the chapter, is a single gal with a busy career as a saleswoman for a swimsuit company. Though she is surrounded by the hottest styles every day, she said she rarely got excited over the new collections. "I just don't *love* wearing a swimsuit," she told me initially. The reason, she said, is that she has always been a little chunky for her frame. To combat that problem, she turned to diets—many of them. "I have been a yo-yo dieter for the last 15 years," she confessed. Because of the failure she experienced on most diets, she suspected a thyroid condition. "I basically begged my general practitioner to test me," she said. Tests showed that while Erica's thyroid and metabolism were indeed sluggish, she didn't have a condition in need of medication. So, the weight issue was back in her hands.

When I first met with Erica, she told me she wanted to lose 35 pounds, adopt good eating habits, train for a 5K run, and increase her metabolism. Because she suspected a sluggish metabolism, I thought it would be best to start there. We took a hard look at her lifestyle. In Erica's busy schedule, she rises at around 7 A.M., arrives at work by 9 A.M., and often gets home as late as 8 P.M. She told me that, generally, she ate large meals for breakfast, lunch, and dinner. Though her meals weren't always necessarily unhealthy and fattening, they were spaced relatively far apart—with lunch at noon and dinner not until 8:30.

Another problem with Erica's meals was a lack of consistency in nutrient content. She might eat high-carb, low-protein meals one day, and high-protein, low-carb meals the next. She wasn't providing her body with consistent amounts of protein to boost her metabolism. It seemed that these widely spaced, nutritionally inconsistent meals were sabotaging her frequent weight-loss efforts.

I advised Erica to eat smaller meals, every three to four hours. This was a new experience for her, and she wasn't so sure it would fit her schedule and actually reduce her cravings. Despite her skepticism, though, she decided to take on the plan whole heartedly.

Erica's first challenge was the timing of her meals. At the beginning of the plan she wasn't eating dinner until 8:30 P.M. So, we tweaked her meal schedule to accommodate that late dinnertime. I asked Erica to start eating a little later in the day, around 9:15 A.M. To address the large lag time between her lunch and dinner, I put Erica on a breakfast-lunch-snack-snack-dinner-snack schedule.

Once the schedule was sorted out, the next challenge was finding the perfect meal and snack choices. Initially, Erica told me she wasn't too psyched about the "B" snacks, having never been a fan of dairy. We discussed what foods did appeal to Erica and quickly came to a compromise. Erica may not be a fan of yogurt or smoothies, but she is a lover of pudding. Easy substitution! Erica was thrilled to learn that calcium-fortified pudding was a friend of the plan. She also acquired some new food faves. "When I first saw the plan, I thought there were some options on there that I would never try," she says, "but now some of those combinations are my favorites." One of the biggest selling points of the plan, she says, is variety. "Even the pickiest eaters can find things they like."

Each weekend, Erica planned her Monday-through-Friday meals and shopped according to the menu. She even made Excel spreadsheets of her menus! She also became familiar with what nutrients the food she was eating offered her. "I definitely read labels now and second-guess my choices. Before, I would go out to dinner and probably go for the first thing that appealed to me. Now I think about how it affects me," she attests. Erica has the plan down to such a science that, she says, she can almost set a clock by when she's going to be hungry. Erica has discovered a feature of the plan that you soon will as well—it enables you to take control of cravings.

Erica also says her new eating habits influenced her motivation to exercise. Whereas she used to go to the gym only on weekdays and only when it wasn't too inconvenient, she started to make exercise mandatory in her week. She adopted a strict schedule of exercise every other day, and even on weekends.

At her first weigh-in, two weeks after the initial visit, she had lost three and three-quarter pounds. By seven weeks, she had lost 12 pounds and was delighted to be able to fit into a pair of Seven jeans, a longtime goal. "I have never done this well," she says. "The plan has changed my life." Erica says the real test will be if she can stick with the plan while she travels for her job. And on an upcoming trip to Florida, she just might be wearing a daring new swimsuit!

Eating for Beauty  3

The 30s Health Prescription for Beautiful Skin and Hair

When I decided to write this book, I thought: yes, 30-something women definitely need an eating plan that keeps us slim and healthy throughout our lives. That much remains true. But one aspect that I felt was often overlooked in popular diet plans—and yet so worthy of discussion—is nutrition advice to keep us looking beautiful for years to come.

Smooth, glowing skin and shiny, healthy hair don't have to be written off as memories of your younger days. Each of us has the ability to keep our physical features in top form at any age. As a matter of fact, one of the most positive aspects of entering your 30s is that you're more likely to invest time and energy in looking your best. Think back: When you were in your 20s, how often did you bother to include specific foods in your diet because they could enhance the appearance of your skin? Or, did it ever occur to you to adopt an antiaging diet as an adjunct to haircuts and colorings, for fabulous-looking hair?

My guess is that you didn't devote much attention to long-term maintenance of a certain level of glamour by eating specific foods and avoiding others. (If you did, you're ahead of the game.) But, as we enter our late 20s and early 30s, we start to detect some not-so-glamorous physical changes. One day we look in the mirror and our eyes are opened by the sight of a line or two around the mouth that didn't exist before. Another day, we are rudely greeted by wrinkles or puffiness under those eyes. Then the hair starts showing gray like never before, or even white. That's when we start to wonder: what can I eat to keep myself looking youthful? Are there foods that can banish wrinkles and make my hair look as healthy as it did five or ten years ago?

Indeed there are. And as it happens, there's no better time than the present to embrace a diet that takes our beauty needs into account.

The 30s Health Prescription: A Recipe for Beauty

Knowing that a healthful diet is about more than just calories, I was determined to create a plan that would provide for the best nutrient-rich meals and snacks for beautiful-looking hair and skin.

You may be familiar with the notion that you are what you eat. Well, you look what you eat, too. And it's not just in your waistline. The foods and beverages you consume are key players when it comes to sustaining long-term health and beauty. Just as certain nutrients protect against diseases (see the lowdown in the next chapter), consuming a well-balanced, antiaging diet is one of your most practical age-defying strategies for maintaining some of your most alluring features: your skin and your hair.

Despite a track record that may include a history of excess sun exposure during your teenage years or habitual pizza and beer binges in your 20s, you don't have to be stuck in an aging zone. Now is the time to take action—by taking advantage of antiaging foods to keep you looking fantastic.

My Plate, My Mirror

A visual analogy can help you understand how it's possible to eat for beauty: Think of your 30s plate as your mirror. Just as a mirror serves as a reflection of your appearance, the foods you eat on this plan offer nutrients that will be feeding your skin, your hair, your nails, and other aspects of your physical being, allowing you to look your best. Consider it a nutritional prescription for beauty. On my plan, you're following a lifestyle of eating not only to achieve a healthy body weight but also to nurture and enhance your finest features.

Feeding Your Skin from Within

When it comes to beautiful-looking skin, what you eat and choose not to eat can affect how your skin looks. The healthy glow, smoothness, and suppleness—even protection against the sun's harmful rays and the possible development of skin cancer—come in part from optimal nutrition, which keeps your skin in its best shape possible. Pampering yourself by ensuring that your skin has optimal amounts of all of the nutrients it requires for its health will keep you looking youthful and ravishing for years to come.

Over the past few years during my nutrition reporting, I've pored over a lot of research on exactly how diet affects the skin. One noteworthy study, published in the *Journal of the American College of Nutrition,* examined the diets of 453 adults living in Sweden, Greece, and Australia. After researchers adjusted for confounding factors such as age and smoking (it contributes to wrinkles), they found that individuals who consumed higher amounts of vegetables, fish, olive oil, and legumes were less prone to skin damage and wrinkling in areas of the skin that were exposed to the sun, compared with those who had a high intake of meat, butter, margarine, high-fat dairy, and sugary foods. In particular, processed red meat, soft drinks, and pastries were associated with extensive skin wrinkling, while foods such as yogurt, beans, green leafy vegetables, asparagus, nuts, olives, cherries, apples, pears, melons, dried fruits, tea, and water—all components of this plan—were associated with less skin aging. All in all, diet accounted for 32 percent of the differences seen in skin wrinkling!

> **Smoke Alert**
>
> While eating the right foods nourishes your skin, smoking does the opposite. Specifically, smoking causes blood vessels to constrict, resulting in decreased perfusion, or blood flow to skin. This can leave skin with a grayish color. Smoking also contributes to wrinkles, including crow's-feet.

Beautiful Skin

The listings of meals and snacks you'll encounter in this book are designed to keep your skin smooth and glowing. In particular, your three meals and "A" snacks offer you optimal amounts of nutrients that will keep your skin in great shape. Below are additional details on nutrients that comprise The 30's Health Prescription for beautiful skin.

Protein for Promoting Healthy Skin

As you now know, consuming an adequate amount of protein is necessary to maximize your resting metabolism. What you may not have realized is that getting enough protein in your diet is also crucial for the maintenance of healthy skin. Proteins are made of amino acids, which form the structure of collagen, the connective tissue that provides support to skin. Additionally, protein-rich foods contain zinc, a mineral necessary for the synthesis of collagen and one that may provide protection against wrinkles. At high levels, zinc may even help improve symptoms of acne. At the other extreme, a deficiency of zinc can result in dermatitis, an inflammation of the skin that can cause itching and redness. Copper, a mineral inherent in protein-rich foods such as shellfish and nuts, is also necessary for collagen synthesis.

Effects of Eating Disorders on Skin

Disordered eating, including starvation diets that result in anorexia nervosa, can precipitate a variety of skin changes, including thin, dry, cold skin that is grayish or pale. Nails become brittle, and hair becomes thin, dry, and dull. Hair also falls out more easily and turns gray more rapidly.

According to Dr. Eliot Ghatan, a dermatologist in private practice in New York City, women who don't get an adequate amount of protein in their diets have unhealthy skin that heals poorly. A junk-food junkie, for example, may fall into this category. A diet of licorice, jelly beans, chocolate bars, and chips is devoid of protein, and therefore, the body is unable to synthesize a sufficient amount of collagen after an injury. The result is the inability of the skin to heal properly. Ghatan remarks that, when performing skin surgery, he can tell the nutritional status of the patient by the thickness of the dermis (middle layer of skin). Without enough protein in your diet, you don't have the building blocks for cells that function in maintaining the integrity of skin.

Junk-food junkies are not the only ones whose eating habits pose a threat in this regard. Many of my 30-something female friends and clients love carbohydrate-rich foods and tend to favor diets with minimal amounts of protein. They're ignoring the fact that loading up on cereal, breads, and pasta for meals (and of course pretzels, chips, and cookies for snacks) takes a toll on the skin. This is in addition to the negative effect that a lack of protein has on metabolism.

When you follow my plan, you will be consuming at least 20 percent of calories from protein, which will provide you with collagen-boosting nutrients for healthy skin.

Antiaging Antioxidants: C, E, and Beta-Carotene

Antioxidants, including vitamin C, vitamin E, and beta-carotene, are crucial for healthy skin. Your skin is made up of layers of fats (lipids) and proteins. These components, while vital for main-

Spotlight on Selenium

Selenium is another antioxidant that can help to rid your body of harmful free radicals that contribute to skin cancer and the aging process. According to the American Academy of Dermatology, selenium is an integral part of the antioxidant glutathione peroxidase, which provides protection against cancers, including skin cancer caused by sun exposure. Selenium also preserves tissue elasticity. The mineral is found in Brazil nuts, tuna, shrimp, turkey, chicken breast, eggs, and brown rice.

taining the integrity of your skin, are particularly vulnerable to damage from the entry of free radicals. Free radicals are highly reactive oxygen molecules generated inside your body from environmental pollutants, smoking, sun exposure, and stress, among other agents. The more free radicals you have roaming around, the greater the opportunity for them to cause cell damage, which can accelerate aging and increase the likelihood of developing skin cancer and other diseases. By maintaining a healthy lifestyle that includes consuming a diet rich in antioxidants, you can help ward off these free radicals and protect your skin and other body cells.

Vitamins C and E and beta-carotene function as antioxidants, meaning they have the ability to ward off free radicals produced by the sun's ultraviolet rays and other pollutants in your environment. This is key because these free radicals have the potential to cause cell damage, which can accelerate aging and increase the likelihood of developing skin cancer and other diseases. Because these antioxidant vitamins play such an important role in maintaining healthy skin, your meals and "A" snacks offer healthy doses of them. In particular, your breakfasts contain lots of berries, which have high levels of these and other protective antioxidants.

Vitamin A Drugs for Skin

Drugs prescribed for acne include Accutane and Retin-A. These are derivatives of vitamin A and should not be taken during pregnancy or if you are planning on becoming pregnant, because in high doses, vitamin A can cause birth defects.

In addition to their shared antioxidant roles, beta-carotene and vitamins C and E have specific roles in maintaining skin health. Beta-carotene, which gets converted to vitamin A in the body, is fundamental to the maintenance of tissues that make up the surface of skin. A deficiency of vitamin A can result in bumpy, rough skin that's covered with fine scales. Aside from keeping skin smooth, this vitamin may also protect against sunburn as recent research suggests. Sources of vitamin A include fortified milk, fish, and egg yolks. Carrots, sweet potatoes, spinach, apricots, and cantaloupe contain beta-carotene.

Foods rich in vitamin C, including broccoli, oranges, peppers, and strawberries, are used by the body for the synthesis of collagen, which provides structure to skin. While rare, a deficiency of vitamin C can cause scurvy, a condition associated with swollen and bleeding gums, loss of teeth, and bleeding underneath the skin. Vitamin E, which is found in nuts, vegetable oils, seeds, avocados, spinach, asparagus, and whole grains, helps to keep skin moist and smooth and protects against wrinkles. As you will see, The 30s Health Prescription contains lots of these skin-friendly foods!

Polyphenols and Skin

Polyphenols are plant-based chemicals that have antioxidant properties similar to those of the vitamins just discussed. In fact, because of their high level of antioxidant activity, the polyphenols present in tea, apples, eggplant, garlic, and onions appear to play a role in protecting the skin against oxidative stress that contributes to aging and disease. To ensure that you are consuming your daily dose of antioxidants, your breakfasts on this plan contain fruits with some of the highest levels of such antioxidants.

Skin Supplements

According to the American Academy of Dermatology, studies have suggested that dietary supplements, including vitamin E, vitamin C, vitamin A, and selenium, offer potential antiaging benefits and protection against skin cancer. Because there is a risk with high doses of these supplements, you should talk to your doctor before taking any of them. And avoid supplements containing high levels of vitamin A if you're planning on becoming pregnant.

Bs for Beautiful Skin

Getting your B vitamins, courtesy of whole grains and fortified cereals, is also important for maintaining youthful skin. Most of your breakfast options and many of your lunches and dinners are rich in these B-containing foods. B vitamins work together with iron to deliver oxygen to skin cells, giving them the support they need to live and multiply into new skin cells.

Niacin (also known as vitamin B_3) is important for healthy skin, and a deficiency of niacin (or the amino acid tryptophan, found in protein-rich foods) causes pellagra, a disease characterized by scaly skin and inflammation. Food sources of niacin include fish, poultry, dairy, and eggs.

Feed Your Skin with Healthful Fats

If you were a yo-yo dieter in your 20s and even your teens, you might have been fat-phobic during some of your dieting phases. Fat is high in calories and therefore should be limited on any diet. (Specifically, 1 gram of either protein or carbohydrate contains 4 calories, while 1 gram of fat contains 9 calories—more than double the amount.) However, eliminating all of the fat from your diet in an effort to shed pounds can wreak havoc on your skin.

Although a "fat-free" diet may sound alluring when it comes to weight loss, it can be detrimental to the health of your skin. In particular, fats known as essential fatty acids (EFAs) help to maintain the oil barrier of skin, which protects the body from fluid loss and infection. The EFAs include polyunsaturated fats such as linoleic acid (an omega-6 fat) and alpha linolenic acid (ALA), an omega-3 fat. These two fats are "essential" because you can get them only from your diet—your body cannot produce them on its own. Once you consume these fats, they get converted into other substances in your body that promote your overall health.

Linoleic acid is found in seeds, nuts, and vegetable oils including sunflower and safflower oils. Alpha linolenic acid is found in walnuts, flaxseed, avocados, and green leafy vegetables such as spinach. According to the Institute of Medicine, a lack of either one of these essential fats will result in symptoms of deficiency, including dermatitis (inflammation of the skin).

A deficiency of EFAs can also lead to eczema, which is characterized by dry, scaly, and rough skin, and brittle nails. Even whiteheads and blackheads can be related to a lack of essential fatty acids. When linoleic acid is lacking, the skin produces a different type of sebum—one that contributes to blackheads and whiteheads and is irritating to the skin.

In addition to the essential omega-3 and omega-6 polyunsaturated fats, monounsaturated fats such as olive and canola oils also play a role in skin health. In fact, in the study on skin wrinkling mentioned at the beginning of the chapter, monounsaturated fats were the only fats that were significantly associated with protection against wrinkles. Remember that skin is composed of fats. Because 25 percent of the fatty acid composition of the epidermis of skin consists of monounsaturated fatty acids, researchers suspect that a high dietary intake of monounsaturated fat may increase the content of monounsaturated fatty acids in the epidermis, which may in turn help to reduce oxidative damage.

Researchers also think that the combination of olive oil and antioxidant-rich vegetables (foods you may consume in a salad, for example) may provide even greater skin protection than antioxidants consumed alone, because the fat in olive oil helps to absorb fat-soluble antioxidant nutrients, such as vitamin E and lycopene.

Butter seems to have the opposite effect. A source of saturated fat, butter was significantly correlated with more skin aging in the previously cited study and explained more than 50 percent of the variance for skin wrinkling when the analysis included only dietary fats.

This plan incorporates many foods rich in healthful fats to maintain beautiful, supple skin. The plan includes a minimum of 20 percent of calories from healthful fats to ward off eczema and other skin problems (20 percent of calories from fat on a 1,400-calorie diet translates to 31 grams of fat).

Fatty Fish for Skin Health

About half of your meal options on this plan contain fish. Fish, especially salmon, herring, sardines, tuna, and trout, are rich sources of omega-3 fats including EPA (eicosapentaenoic acid) and DHA (docoasahexaenoic acid). In high amounts, these fatty acids have been shown to reduce internal inflammation that is associated with psoriasis, a skin disorder often characterized by white scales with redness surrounding them. One study published in the *Journal of the American Academy of Dermatology* found that when given intravenously, a combination of EPA and DHA resulted in an improvement of the disorder and concluded that it is an effective treatment of plaque-type psoriasis. Other studies have reported similar results.

Psoriasis is not the only skin issue related to omega-3 intake. Some researchers say that acne may be an effect of insufficient intake of omega-3 fats in relation to omega-6 fats. This type of imbalance can cause inflammation, leading to blocked pores and thus to overproduction of oil. (Diet and acne are further discussed in the following section.)

Not-So-Sweet News About Sugar and Your Skin

There's more reason than just avoiding extra calories to keep your sweet tooth in check. Sugar and sugary foods may also be involved with deterioration in skin health, through a process known as glycosylation of proteins. When a high level of sugar is present in the bloodstream, sugars can attach to protein fibers in collagen and produce compounds called advanced glycation end products (AGEs). As their name implies, AGEs make skin less resilient and contribute to wrinkles and sagging.

What's more, despite conventional wisdom, recent research has suggested that sugary and refined carbohydrates contribute to acne. Loren Cordain, Ph.D., a professor of health and exercise science at Colorado State University, has studied the topic extensively and says acne can be traced to diet in several ways. For example, highly refined carbohydrates such as white bread and sugars cause a spike in insulin, which increases production of hormones known as androgens. High levels of androgens cause sebaceous glands in the skin to secrete excess amounts of oil, which contributes to acne. Eating these foods may increase other factors in your bloodstream that contribute to clogged pores.

Along related lines, an Australian study exemplified how a diet low in these refined carbohydrates can help to treat acne. In the study, published in the *Asia Pacific Journal of Clinical Nutrition*, a low-glycemic-load diet comprising high levels of protein with minimal amounts of

Water Break

Aim to drink lots of water on a daily basis. Adequate hydration will help to keep skin soft, smooth, and moist. Also, when your skin is hydrated, wrinkles are less noticeable!

sugar was shown to significantly decrease the average number of facial acne lesions, thereby alleviating the severity of acne symptoms.

Your best course for optimal skin health is to limit your intake of refined carbohydrates and sugary foods, but you can serve yourself portion-controlled amounts of these foods in your meals and as "C" snacks. This way, you can enjoy these treats while avoiding overconsumption, which can lead to wrinkles and breakouts.

Caffeine and Alcohol

Caffeine causes water loss from your body, including your skin. If your intake of caffeine is high, your skin may not look plump. I recommend limiting caffeine to 300 milligrams (mg) per day—that's about two large cups of caffeinated coffee, or three small—and including green tea as an alternative beverage in your diet. Green tea has less caffeine than coffee; it also contains antioxidants that may protect against skin cancer. (More information on green tea is included in the discussion of sunscreen later in the chapter.)

Alcohol has a diuretic effect, so excess alcohol can dehydrate your skin. (Have you ever woken up after a late night of drinking and noticed that your skin appeared really wrinkled?) Alcohol can also cause skin to turn red through its ability to dilate blood vessels. Dr. Ghatan points out that consuming just one alcoholic beverage can dilate blood vessels, causing redness and flushing on the face. If you suffer from psoriasis or rosacea, it's best to avoid alcohol, because it can exacerbate symptoms of these skin conditions.

My Skin Story

I've always been told I have beautiful, porcelain-looking skin, but as I've entered my 30s, I haven't felt so fortunate watching fine lines slowly appear on my face. I'm not saying that everyone notices, but I can assure you, when I look in the mirror, I see them! What I've learned, however, in addition to the importance of following a good skin care regimen, is that I can eat to keep my skin looking healthy and radiant. I eat lots of fish, I drink lots of water, and I focus on olive oil and other vegetable oils as my main source of fat in meals. I rarely eat red meat or fried foods. In fact, I probably eat these foods maybe three times a year, if that often. I also limit my intake of alcohol and caffeine. I'll typically have one strong cup of coffee in the morning (two on TV mornings to get me awake at 4 A.M.). When I go out with friends, I'll have either a glass of wine or a martini. I can't say the fine lines on my face have disappeared, but I can tell you that my skin feels smooth and soft and is in great shape!

The Skinny Trap

As a 30-something concerned with maintaining good health and beauty for myself and my peers, I was eager to talk with dermatologists to see what they had to say regarding a diet prescription for youthful-looking skin. All agreed that a healthy diet was critical for maintaining smooth, glowing skin. The comments of Dr. Roberta Sengelmann, a dermatologist in her 30s and the director of dermatologic and cosmetic surgery at Washington University School of Medicine in St. Louis, were particularly appropriate for us. She told me that in her private practice, she's observed that many of her female patients in their late 20s and 30s who are on low-cal, fad diets lack supple skin. They are so concerned with limiting calories and avoiding certain foods that their skin suffers from their omitting important vitamins and fats. She added, "My patients who have healthy, glowing, beautiful skin are not the ones who are supermodel skinny, but rather, they are the ones who look *healthy* and follow a nutritious, well-balanced diet."

Sengelmann, who is a long-haired, 38-year-old blonde, understands our issues: "Believe me, I know. We haven't necessarily met the right guy yet; we're getting married a bit later in life; we're under a ton of stress; we're looking into fertility issues—and, at the same time, we want to stay beautiful." But Roberta confirmed for me something I've known since I started studying nutrition and how it affects our beauty: staying youthful is not necessarily about which cream to buy, or which peel you should undergo. Rather, it's about committing to a healthy diet and lifestyle.

Unlike fad diets, which frequently eliminate nutritious foods, the program I offer is a nutrient-dense, antiaging diet. That's what sets it apart from the rest. When following it, you will get the weight-loss results you're after and the calories you do consume will fuel your beauty—starting in your 30s and for years to come!

Attention: All Sun Worshippers

For many of us, during our teens and 20s, when we went to the beach for spring break or other vacations, coming back with a tan was top priority. That meant that days at the shore were filled with multiple applications of oily sunscreen. I still wince at the memory of the time I was in St. Martin and didn't get as "dark" as I wanted to on the first day after using a sunscreen with the recommended sun protection factor (SPF) of 15. On the second day, out of mild frustration, I engaged in a behavior typical of my generation: I slathered on oil-based lotion with an SPF of 6 and sat out for a few hours. Basically, I fried. The next morning, my eyes were so swollen and distorted that I thought I had permanent damage. I'm embarrassed to tell this incident, but I do because it has value as a vivid reminder of the damage the sun can do to our most precious features, especially our skin.

Luckily, I learned my lesson and have taken care to avoid burns. I still love the feel of the sun on my face in the summertime, but knowing the extent of damage and photoaging that the sun can cause to skin (about 90 percent of skin aging is due to exposure to the sun's ultraviolet light), I make an effort to stay out of direct sunlight. When I do go to the beach or lie by the pool, I put on SPF 30 and limit my exposure to a half hour tops.

Skin Saboteurs and 30s Health Prescription Solutions

To help you counteract the first visible signs of aging and keep your skin glowing, let's review some skin saboteurs and their solutions.

Saboteur: A very low-fat diet
Solution: Aim for a minimum of 20 percent of calories from healthy fats, including fatty fish, nuts, and olive and vegetable oils.

Saboteur: A diet lacking protein (for example, eating carbs all day)
Solution: Get at least three ounces (21 grams) of protein per meal, or at least 20 percent of total calories from protein sources.

Saboteur: Too much caffeine
Solution: Limit caffeine to 300 mg per day, and alternate with water and green tea.

Saboteur: Too much alcohol
Solution: Limit yourself to no more than one alcoholic beverage per day.

Safe Suntanning

This prescription for safe suntanning is based on recommendations from dermatologists and advice from the American Academy of Dermatology.

1. **Go for SPF 15 or above.** Regardless of your skin type, you should use a sunscreen with an SPF of at least 15. To give you an idea of what an SPF of 15 means: if you're fair-skinned and you typically turn red after 10 minutes of sun exposure, with an SPF of 15, it would take 150 minutes—or 15 times longer—before you would burn. An SPF of 15 blocks 93 percent of the sun's ultraviolet (UV) rays, and an SPF of 30 blocks 97 percent. An SPF of 2 blocks only 50 percent of UV rays.
2. **Use UVA/UVB ("broad spectrum protection") sunscreens.** UVB rays are the primary cause of sunburn and skin cancer, but UVA rays penetrate deeply into the skin (they can even penetrate windows) and are harmful as well. You need protection against both regions of the UV spectrum.
3. **Consider physical versus chemical blocks.** The actual blocks used in sunscreens can be either physical or chemical. Chemical blocks go by names such as Parsol 1789, salicylates, cinnamates, and benzophenones. Some dermatologists prefer physical blocks such as zinc oxide or titanium dioxide, because they reflect the light away instead of absorbing it into the skin. Physical blocks may also be preferable for people with skin allergies.
4. **Don't skimp when applying sunscreen.** In addition to choosing the right type of sunscreen, it is important to use an adequate amount. The American Academy of Dermatology says one ounce, enough to fill a shot glass, is considered the amount needed to cover the exposed areas of the body properly. Sunscreen should be reapplied every two hours, or after swimming or perspiring heavily. (Water-resistant sunscreens may lose their effectiveness after 80 minutes in the water, so it's necessary to reapply.)

Topical Antioxidants

To protect yourself from the sun, should you be feeding your face and skin with topical antioxidants? That's the question you may find yourself asking when you look at all of the vitamin-fortified sunscreens on shelves now.

At least one study suggests that a combination of vitamins C and E provides additional protection against damage caused by the sun's ultraviolet rays. The study, from Duke University, found that when pigskin was irradiated with ultraviolet light, the combination of vitamins C and E provided a fourfold protection against sunburn, compared with a placebo cream. Plus, the vitamins provided protection against DNA damage in skin cells that can lead to mutations that cause skin cancer.

How do the vitamins relate to the SPF? Generally speaking, you can improve the SPF of sunscreen with the addition of vitamins C and E by a factor of 1 to 4. In other words, if you have an SPF of 15, you might get an SPF of 19 with the vitamins added.

Avoiding Sunscreen for D? Don't.

You may have heard that not wearing sunscreen can help you meet your needs for vitamin D. While it is true that about 20 to 40 minutes of sun exposure without sunscreen, three times per week, can meet your D requirements, the American Academy of Dermatology does not recommend this and says that even the most effective sunscreens on the market let enough UV light through to allow for adequate vitamin D synthesis. If you're still worried about not getting enough vitamin D when wearing sunscreen, take a multivitamin, or drink low-fat milk as your "B" snack (it's fortified with D).

Protecting Your Skin from Within—After You've Been Out in the Sun

Foods such as watermelon, cantaloupe, carrots, tomatoes, and mangoes also may help to protect against sunburn. These foods are rich in carotenoids, including beta-carotene and lycopene. A recent study published in the *Journal of Nutrition* revealed that daily supplementation with carotenoids, including beta-carotene, lutein, and lycopene, helped to decrease redness in skin when skin was exposed to ultraviolet light.

Other research has revealed that EGCG, a substance in green tea, protects against DNA damage that could lead to skin tumors, when human skin cells are exposed to ultraviolet light. EGCG is an antioxidant that can help to rid the body of free radicals generated by the sun's ultraviolet rays. (As mentioned earlier, free radicals can cause damage to cells, which can ultimately lead to skin cancer.) During the hot summer months, try iced green tea instead of iced coffee.

Melissa's Story

Melissa was always stick-thin with flawless skin and beautiful hair. She was one of "those girls" who never dieted and never broke 115 pounds. Even at 5'8", a size 2–4 was a perfect fit. But then came baby. At age 21, just out of college, Melissa had her first baby *and* her first major weight gain. A whopping 60 pounds found its way onto her previously rail-thin frame. And though she lost about 30 pounds after giving birth, her new size became a 12. Within a few years came baby number two and though she lost all of that pregnancy weight, she couldn't get past a size 10 at 155 pounds.

After two kids, a demanding career, and the age of 30 staring her in the face, she decided she was due for "Melissa time." Having had her first baby at age 21, Melissa hadn't felt physically attractive since her teens. "I want to feel good about myself—feel young and sexy again! Not a washed-up married mother of two little boys," she said. Melissa was searching for something to jump-start her into a healthy, beautiful 30.

To take control of her health, Melissa sought the help of The 30s Health Prescription. She was serious about achieving results, so I had faith that she would make her goals happen. But first we had to tackle a big obstacle—her nutritional mind-set. Melissa's diet was not conducive to reaching that goal. With eggplant parmigiana or pizza as typical dinners and M&Ms and Snickers as midmorning snacks, a new way of eating was a vital place to start.

Melissa was thrilled to see that the food choices on the plan were all friendly and familiar to her. She could still have her eggplant dish. But the plan's version included *whole wheat* pasta with eggplant. Instead of Snickers as a late-morning snack at work, she goes for her "A" snack—a bag of carrots. One cup of low-fat chocolate pudding as a "C" snack satisfies her chocolate cravings. She realized that customizing the plan to meet her tastes would make it work for her.

Melissa says the plan works for her because it is so simple. The essentials of the plan—the "ABC's" and the "one-third" approach to her plate—were easy guidelines to follow. Once the guidelines were firmly rooted in her, it was all about control.

Now, two months into the plan, she has dropped down to 135 pounds. She says, "I can't remember the last time I went overboard eating out. I'm also back to working out two to three times a week and feel great."

Melissa is ecstatic that she has gone down to size 8 pants! And, more important, she feels sexier in them. "I call my 30s the decade of me. I don't want to go to the beach and have people say, 'She shouldn't be wearing that bathing suit.' I want to be the one who everyone stares at and says, 'Wow, she looks great for a mother of two!'"

Eating for Healthy Hair

We might notice that as we enter our late 20s and 30s, our hair texture and color start to change. Many of us will experience our first gray hairs, others may find white hair in certain spots, and still others will find that their hair lacks the shine it used to have. "I have more and more gray hairs popping up from nowhere," says Nicole, a busy, stressed 35-year-old New Yorker. "I have been pulling them out," she admits, "which I'm sure can't be good! And when I wash my hair, I am finding more and more hair in the shower trap afterward! I am now trying to wash it less and wear it in a ponytail most of the time."

It's normal for your hair texture and color to change a bit with time. But, as with your skin, there are ways to feed your hair the nutrition it needs to keep it looking its best. I'm not telling you to stop coloring your hair, or relaxing it, if you love how it looks, but I do want to share with you how simple nutritional adjustments can make great improvements in the health of your hair.

Nutrient Deficiencies and Hair Problems

Protein and iron are musts for healthy hair. Thirty-something women at greatest risk for diet-related hair changes include those on high-carbohydrate diets, who

Maximizing Iron in Your Diet

Women 19 to 50 years old require 18 mg of iron each day; needs increase to 27 mg during pregnancy. Women who are at risk for iron deficiency include those who lose a lot of blood (and therefore iron) during menstruation, very strict dieters, vegetarians, and endurance athletes. If you feel you may be at risk for iron deficiency, follow these tips:

1. **Choose meals with chicken, fish, and lean beef.** These foods are sources of heme iron, which is better absorbed than nonheme iron, the only type of iron found in plant-based foods and in dairy and eggs. Oysters and clams are good sources as well.

2. **Go for iron-fortified cereals.** Whole Grain Total (18 mg of iron per three-quarters-cup serving) and Multi-Grain Cheerios (17 mg per one-cup serving) are excellent fortified options. Fortified

oatmeal is another good source.

3. **Have an orange as your breakfast fruit, along with your fortified cereals.** The vitamin C in oranges can increase the amount of nonheme iron absorbed. According to the University of California, Berkeley, you can triple the amount of iron absorbed from a vegetarian meal by adding 75 mg of vitamin C.

4. **Cook in iron pots.** The iron leaches into the food, boosting the amount of iron in your meal.

5. **Drink coffee or tea *between* meals (not with meals).** Compounds including tannins in tea and polyphenols in coffee may inhibit nonheme iron absorption.

6. **Don't take calcium supplements at the same time you take your iron-containing multi.** Calcium and iron compete for absorption in the body.

may not be consuming an adequate amount of protein; crash dieters, who lose a lot of weight in a short amount of time; and vegans, whose diets lack animal protein from all sources, putting them at risk for insufficient intakes of iron and vitamin B_{12}.

Protein for Pretty Hair

While you may be consuming an adequate amount of calories, if your diet is very low in protein, your hair can lose its color or become dull. According to Dr. Martha H. Stipanuk, a Cornell University professor who studies the effects of protein malnutrition, if you're consuming less than 7 percent of calories from protein, you can undergo changes in hair pigmentation. You may start to see pale hair or have a band of hair that is a different color. (Seven percent of protein calories on a 1,400-calorie diet is equivalent to 25 grams of protein, or about three and a half ounces of fish.)

If you're following a prolonged liquid diet, for example, you may be lacking sufficient protein and calories, which can show itself through changes in hair color. Likewise, if you're consuming too many carbohydrates at the expense of protein—for instance, if your daily diet consists of a muffin for breakfast; pasta for lunch; and pizza for dinner—you are engaging in eating behavior that is hazardous to your hair. Beyond changes in color, not getting enough protein can result in thin, dry hair. And forget about shine—hair will lack luster too.

Iron: An Important Hair Nutrient

If your diet is low in iron, your hair may suffer consequences. Iron is a mineral that promotes hair growth. Even if you are not clinically anemic, you can experience hair loss simply from not getting enough iron in your diet. (Nails can become fragile and brittle as well.) Iron deficiency can also leave you with lusterless, dry, brittle hair. These symptoms may be due to changes in the production of keratins—proteins integral to hair formation.

Lose Pounds Too Quickly, Lose Hair

Losing weight too rapidly can also result in hair loss. If you lose more than 10 percent of your body weight over a couple of months (e.g., more than 15 pounds if you weighed 150), you can lose hair. The condition, known as telogen effluvium, is typically accompanied by diets that lack protein. According to Marianne O'Donoghue, M.D., associate professor of dermatology at Rush University Medical Center in Chicago, the actual hair loss may occur about three months after one drastically sheds pounds. The hair will usually grow back within about six months, or when one's weight stabilizes.

On The 30s Health Prescription, you should be losing weight at a rate of one to two pounds per week. If you're losing more than this, I recommend switching to a higher calorie level. In addition to putting yourself at risk for hair loss, you are more likely to have difficulty sustaining your weight loss.

Healthy Hair

Whether you have blond or brown hair, straight or curly hair, The 30s Health Prescription will help keep it healthy and shiny. Just as a balanced diet helps in maintaining smooth and glowing skin, eating nutrient-rich meals and snacks can help keep your hair looking its best, whatever the color and texture. The 30s Health Prescription supplies you with nutrient-rich foods that are beneficial for hair health. For example, the whole grains and proteins in your meals are excellent sources of vitamins and minerals that are necessary for maintaining healthy hair, including B vitamins, iron, and zinc.

Avoid Excess A

Vitamin A, compliments of liver, milk, eggs, cheese, and yogurt, is needed for the maintenance of a healthy scalp; however, excess amounts of preformed vitamin A can cause toxicity, leading to a loss of hair or coarse hair. According to the National Academy of Sciences, the safe upper limit is 10,000 IU of vitamin A daily. One eight-ounce glass of fortified skim milk has 500 IU of vitamin A; one medium hard-boiled egg has 258 IU. One ounce of Swiss and extra-sharp cheddar cheese each have 300 IU. Four ounces of cooked chicken liver has 16,300 IU.

Foods Rich in Hair Nutrients

The foods in your plan that are rich in hair nutrients include fish, shellfish, chicken, and turkey. In addition to being excellent sources of protein, these foods contain tyrosine, which is an amino acid—a building block of protein—that is responsible for hair color. Copper, a mineral found in fish and shellfish, also contributes to hair color, and a deficiency can cause changes in the pigment of hair. Omega-3 fats in fish (especially salmon) play a role in keeping your hair healthy, and consuming an adequate intake of iron—found in lean meats, fish, and other protein-rich foods—can protect against hair shedding.

Also guard against a deficiency of vitamin C, which can cause hair breakage. Consuming one cup of cooked broccoli will give you your daily dose of C. Biotin, a B vitamin found in soybeans, mushrooms, peanut butter, and egg yolks, is also important for healthy hair, and a deficiency can result in hair thinning and loss of hair color. Zinc is critical as well, and a deficiency can cause hair loss and even a loss of eyelashes. Oysters and crabmeat are prime sources of zinc.

Your breakfasts and snacks on this plan contain vital hair nutrients. For example, fortified breakfast cereals provide vitamin B_{12} and bananas provide vitamin B_6. These B vitamins, along with foods rich in folic acid (fortified cereals, strawberries, oranges, and spinach), help to form red blood cells, which bring oxygen to the hair and allow it to grow at a healthy rate.

You will be feeding your hair nutrients that will keep it shiny and healthy. Still, to give you some nutritional insurance, I recommend a multivitamin/multimineral supplement as part of your plan, to protect against any possible deficiencies associated with changes in hair color or hair loss.

Eating for Optimal Health

(4)

The 30s Health Prescription for Preventing Disease

By now, it should be obvious that this plan is no quick fix or fad diet. It's a long-term plan for good health and beauty that takes *your* unique lifestyle needs into account. Whether you've seen a family member battle heart disease or cancer, or received a diagnosis of high cholesterol or other medical condition, concern for your health begins to take center stage in this fourth decade of life.

I remember the time when I was hired several years ago to work on a nutrition project involving 14 female magazine editors in their late 20s and 30s, most of whom specialized in health and fitness. My task was to give each editor a nutritional assessment, based on her current eating patterns and lifestyle habits. I asked each of them what her top two goals were, as I usually do with clients. The editors spanned the country and had different lifestyles, needs, and stressors. Regardless of what they were encountering at the moment, all of the women said they wanted to master an eating plan that would help them shed pounds *and* increase their chances of living a long, healthy life.

It was right at this point in my career that I was determined to formulate a plan that would encompass health,
beauty, and weight issues related to food. I frequently pon-
dered: What would be the best diet for a woman in her 30s
and beyond? What would be the major obstacles to women
in achieving their goals? And what would an eating plan that
addresses these issues look like?

I figured it would be best to create a pattern of eating that
would be simplistic, in light of all the details with which 30-
something women are consumed in their daily lives. I came
up with the thirds ratio for plates—one-third protein, one-
third vegetables, and one-third grains. This ratio would allow
for a moderate amount of protein and carbohydrates, while
offering a high amount of fiber and vitamins. For snacks,
women would need antiaging, bone-building, and comfort
foods. These snack foods would provide nutrients for disease
prevention, beauty, and, of course, comfort. All meals and
snacks would be calorie controlled to help women slim down
or simply keep their weight in check.

Whitney's Story

I met with Whitney, one of the magazine editors in the nutrition project, to share my new plan with her. We reviewed
several meal and snack options that would fit into her busy
work schedule while meeting her nutritional requirements.

After starting the plan, Whitney told me she liked the fact
that she was eating a healthful, balanced diet—something
that previously fell by the wayside in the midst of her tight
deadlines. The simplicity of the plan had much to do with
her enthusiasm. Whitney enjoyed counting her "A," "B," and
"C" snacks throughout the day, knowing she was fueling herself with the mental energy her job demanded. A priority
for Whitney was health, which fit perfectly with the plan's
main focus. The knowledge that she was eating to ward off

diseases, she said, was empowering. She commented, "I'm pretty health conscious, but sometimes keeping all the information straight in your head—calories, fat, fiber, you name it—when you're hungry and then actually choosing what to eat can be hard. When you think of snacks in terms of ABC's, it's so much simpler, yet still keeps you mindful of your health. That it helped me lose weight was just a bonus."

The time I spent developing this plan for Whitney and many others has been well worth it. Every woman who has experienced success on the plan is thrilled that she can lose weight without following a fad diet that may harm her health. Instead, women are eating to ward off disease, in addition to shedding pounds. Now you too will be armed with delicious antiaging, bone-building, and disease-fighting foods. I'm talking about meals and snacks that will help protect you against osteoporosis, heart disease, diabetes, cancer, and more. And I am confident you will love them!

Protection Against Osteoporosis

Ever since I was a child, I avoided yogurt. I'm not sure why, but it was one of those foods I never had a longing for. I enjoyed milk but really never had it, either, outside the boundaries of a cereal bowl. Then when I entered college, I learned about the importance of having strong bones to protect myself against osteoporosis. I remember thinking: I *need* to get more calcium in my diet.

Apparently, I'm not alone: ninety percent of women who responded to a recent survey from the American Dietetic Association said they believe calcium is important to their health, yet nearly half don't get enough. Research tells us that the average calcium intake among women is about 625 milligrams (mg) per day, far short of the recommended intake of 1,000 mg for 30-somethings (and 1,200 for women over 50). Moreover, for one-quarter of women, eating or drinking milk products isn't an option, because they either can't tolerate them or don't like them. In light of this formidable barrier to calcium consumption, I was eager to find some of the yummiest calcium-fortified foods around. I have worked in my favorites as part of your "B" snack list.

The Calcium Connection

Calcium, along with vitamin D and magnesium, is critical for the health of your bones at this time in your life. When you hit your 30s, your peak bone mass is achieved. What this means is that *your body begins to break down bone faster than new bone is formed*. In fact, from age 35 until menopause, you will lose about 1 percent of your bone mass each year. Simply, you become less efficient at building bone, and you need to do everything you can to keep your bones healthy. If you don't get enough calcium from your diet, your bones release calcium into the bloodstream and become deprived of the mineral. Over time, this can cause bones to weaken and become brittle, putting you at greater risk for osteoporosis later in life.

As mentioned earlier, our daily recommended intake for calcium is 1,000 mg per day. Don't worry about counting milligrams, though. On this plan, your antiaging breakfasts and

My Thoughts on Multis

Even if you're following this diet to a T, I recommend taking a multivitamin/multimineral supplement. A multi will provide you with nutrition insurance on days when your best-laid food plans go awry, helping you to fill in nutritional gaps. Additionally, research is revealing that multis may offer health benefits such as improved memory and protection against heart attacks and colorectal cancer.

A few pertinent notes:

- When choosing a multivitamin/multimineral, look for 100 percent of the recommended value for vitamins and minerals. More than this is not necessary and can be harmful in some cases.
- You won't meet your calcium needs in a multi and will need to take a

separate calcium supple-
ment if you're not getting
enough of the mineral
from your diet.
- Look for a multi that
contains no more than
3,000 international units
(IU) of preformed vitamin
A (i.e., retinol). The higher
the percentage of beta-
carotene, the better.
An excess of vitamin A
can be toxic to the liver,
though. High levels have
also been associated with
bone fractures in post-
menopausal women.

I recommend taking your
multi with breakfast, because
taking it without food can
cause stomach upset. And
if you are taking a calcium
supplement, take it at a
different time during the day,
because calcium competes
with minerals in your multi
for absorption in the body.

"B" snacks each contain 25 percent of your daily needs (that's 250 mg), and each day packs in 100 percent—1,000 mg—of calcium. If you find yourself skipping calcium-rich foods, though, or simply want insurance to cover you for your daily requirements, take a calcium supplement.

Calcium Supplements

If you're having trouble getting in your "B" snacks and other calcium-rich foods at breakfast and throughout the day, it's a good idea to consider a calcium supplement. Calcium carbonate and calcium citrate are two popular types you're likely to see on store shelves.

Calcium carbonate is found in supplements such as Caltrate (600 mg calcium per tablet). Per gram, calcium carbonate offers more calcium. In other words, compared with the citrate kind, a higher percentage of calcium is present in the carbonate version. Because of this, the pills may be a bit smaller and are typically less expensive.

Calcium citrate is found in brands such as Citracal, which contains either 250 mg or 315 mg of calcium per tablet, depending on the formula. Some studies suggest that calcium citrate is better absorbed than calcium carbonate, but this is really most important for elderly individuals who may not be producing an adequate amount of stomach acid, which can make it difficult to absorb the mineral.

When making a decision about calcium supplements, the most important factor is to choose the one you are most likely to use. If you don't like to swallow pills, chewable versions of calcium are available, such as Viactiv and Healthy Indulgence. Each one contains 500 mg of calcium (from calcium carbonate). Note, though, that they do contribute some calories to your diet. Another source of calcium (again, the carbonate kind) is Tums. Each maximum-strength Tums contains 400 mg of calcium. I often recommend Tums as a calcium source for women who are suffering from heartburn during pregnancy.

Whichever calcium supplement you choose, don't take it at the same time you take a multivitamin/multimineral supplement, because calcium competes with other minerals for absorption (iron and zinc, for example). Additionally, if you are taking more than 500 mg of calcium from supplements each day (which I recommend if you're not consuming any calcium-rich foods), divide your total dosage into two separate doses for better absorption. Taking calcium with meals will also boost absorption; however, avoid taking calcium

Delicious Calcium-Rich Foods

As concern for my bones loomed larger in my late 20s, I started searching for the tastiest calcium-rich foods I could find. It seemed that more and more companies were coming out with foods and beverages for the calcium-conscious consumer. Here are some that I deemed winners:

1. Calcium-fortified chocolate soy milk

2. Skim latte with sugar-free vanilla syrup

3. Quaker Oatmeal Nutrition for Women (50 percent of your daily calcium needs per packet)

4. Swiss Miss Fat Free Hot Cocoa Mix with Calcium

5. Café au lait

6. Silk Live! Soy smoothie

7. Stonyfield Farm Organic Low-Fat Yogurt Smoothie

8. Pria Complete Nutrition Bar

9. Luna bar

10. Glenny's Low-Fat Soy Crisps (BBQ)

11. Swiss Miss low-fat chocolate pudding fortified with calcium

12. Turkey Hill's frozen yogurt and no-sugar-added ice cream fortified with calcium

13. Propel Calcium (fitness water)—one bottle has approximately 300 mg of calcium, equivalent to 30 percent of your daily needs

14. Healthy Indulgence milk or dark chocolate calcium supplements (25 calories each)

supplements with foods containing phytates or oxalates (more on this later). And be sure to drink fluids with calcium supplements to avoid constipation.

Avoiding Vitamin D Deficiency

Equally important in protecting against osteoporosis is getting enough vitamin D, which helps to absorb the calcium we consume. Without an adequate amount of D, our bodies can't make use of the calcium we take in. It seems that as we get older, we may not be getting enough D, especially because our needs increase through the years. In fact, according to a recent study from Columbia University Medical Center, in New York, more than half (up to 52 percent) of North American women currently receiving treatment for osteoporosis have insufficient levels of vitamin D.

Although it's true that sun exposure can provide vitamin D, the vitamin is best synthesized in skin that is not protected with sunscreen—something I don't recommend. So, what should 30-something women do to meet our D needs? For one, I recommend including fat-free or low-fat milk in your diet at least once each day, either as a "B" snack or as part of your breakfast. (If you are lactose intolerant, try Lactaid or soy milk fortified with calcium and D.) Milk is one of the few food sources of vitamin D, so this is somewhat of a no-brainer. Additionally, focus on other foods rich in D, such as salmon, fortified cereals, and, on occasion, egg yolks. If you feel you're not consuming an adequate amount of D from foods, a multivitamin (or calcium supplement) with 200 IU will allow you to meet your daily D needs. To play it safe, avoid more than 1,000 IU of vitamin D.

Fruits and Vegetables for Your Bones

Here's another benefit of consuming fruits and vegetables that I'm psyched to share with you: they may play a role in keeping your bones healthy! According to a study in the *American Journal of Clinical Nutrition*, fruits and vegetables may help to prevent osteoporosis. The authors of the study found that lifelong consumption of fruits and vegetables (as well as high intakes of potassium and magnesium) were determinants of bone mineral density in older women and men. Specifically, produce may help keep your bones healthy by *preserving* bone mineral density. It's thought that fruits and vegetables help to neutralize stomach acid produced during digestion—without depending on the buffering effects of the bone minerals, which can compromise the integrity of bone.

Got Milk, Lose Weight?

Is there a connection between calcium and weight loss? One recent study disclosed a possible link. The study found that women who consumed 500 fewer calories and ate three to four servings of dairy foods each day as part of their diet, including milk, yogurt, and cheese, lost an average of 24 pounds, or 11 percent of their body weight, over six months. Those who cut back on calories and took a calcium supplement (800 mg) lost 19 pounds, or 9 percent of their body weight. And women who cut calories and consumed only 400 mg of calcium lost 15 pounds, or 6 percent of their body weight. As you can see, women who consumed the most dairy and calcium lost almost double the amount of weight lost by those who consumed the least.

Another recent study, from Purdue University, found that normal-weight women who consumed three to four servings of dairy each day over the course of a year burned more fat and calories from a meal than women who consumed less than three servings of dairy per day.

Both studies were funded by the dairy industry. Whether or not independent studies confirm a role for calcium in weight loss, the bottom line is this: It's important to consume 1,000 mg of calcium daily to keep your bones strong. For now, consider any potential weight loss effects from calcium as a bonus.

Protection Against Heart Disease: My Top Five

If heart disease runs in your family, you're probably starting to worry about it. Now is the time you start thinking: I have to do something about my cholesterol, my weight, my lack of exercise, my ice-cream-filled nights! Take Robin, a 33-three-year-old woman whose most serious concern is heart disease. She explained, "My father had a heart attack at age 34—just one year older than I am—and he recently had a triple bypass. My cholesterol runs very high, and I will probably have to go on medication after I have a family."

Being overweight certainly puts us at greater risk for heart disease, the number one killer of both women and men. Carrying excess body fat, especially around the waist, is an independent risk factor for the disease. A family history of heart disease, high cholesterol, high blood pressure, diabetes, and uncontrolled stress are other significant risk factors. Further, smokers have more than twice the risk for heart attack as nonsmokers and are more likely to die if they suffer a heart attack.

Eating a healthful, balanced diet can keep these risk factors in check, while decreasing the chances for disease. I'm going to arm you with heart-healthy foods, as I did for Robin, that can help decrease your risk factors for heart disease and stroke. These foods have been distributed throughout your plan.

All fruits, vegetables, whole grains, lean proteins, and healthy fats are fundamental to your 30s plan for protection against diseases. However, in the following sections, I'm shining the spotlight on the top five foods with special heart-protective benefits. You may include these foods in your meals and "A" snacks if you're concerned specifically about heart disease and stroke.

1. Berries

You might have been hearing a lot about berries lately—and wondering why they're so hot. Berries, including strawberries, blueberries, raspberries, and blackberries, are rich in

Bone-Busting Nutrients

Phytates and oxalates in foods can interfere with calcium absorption in the body. Phytates are substances contained in wheat bran, beans, and peas, and oxalates exist in spinach, rhubarb, beet greens, and almonds. It's best to eat your breakfasts and "B" snacks separately from these foods, so your body can take full advantage of the calcium present in your meals and snacks.

Other nutrients in high amounts can interfere with bone health. For example, excessive amounts of protein and sodium can cause calcium to be lost through the kidneys. (You don't need to worry about consuming an excess of these nutrients on your plan.) Additionally, drinking caffeinated beverages can cause some

antiaging nutrients, offering protection against heart disease and other areas of aging such as cancer and memory loss. Blueberries, raspberries, and blackberries in particular are loaded with antioxidants. These berries are among foods with the highest levels of antioxidants, according to the U.S. Department of Agriculture (USDA). These natural chemicals may prevent the oxidation of low-density lipoprotein (LDL) cholesterol, a process that causes plaque buildup in artery walls, which can lead to a heart attack or stroke.

calcium to be excreted in urine—approximately 5 mg of calcium is lost for every 150 mg of caffeine. This amount of caffeine is found in one large cup of coffee or about three 12-ounce cans of caffeinated soda.

To offset calcium losses from caffeinated beverages, it's important to consume an adequate amount of calcium in your daily diet. By following this plan, you'll consume a minimum of 1,000 mg of calcium each day. However, if you are skipping "B" snacks, and not consuming other calcium-fortified foods, I recommend adding a calcium supplement to your diet. Also, it's wise to add about two tablespoons of skim or low-fat milk to your caffeinated coffee or tea.

In addition to antioxidants, berries contain folate, potassium, and vitamin C. Berries also offer a fiber boost—blueberries and strawberries have close to 4 grams of fiber per cup; raspberries have 8 grams—or double the amount! Because they impart a sweet taste to cereals and yogurt, it was an easy decision to include all types of berries as part of your breakfasts on The 30s Health Prescription.

2. Oatmeal

When it comes to protection against heart disease, oats are on the front line because of their cholesterol-lowering effect. Oats contain beta-glucan, a type of soluble fiber (meaning it dissolves in water) that has been shown to lower both total and LDL (harmful) cholesterol levels. Oats' ability to lower LDL is so great that the Food and Drug Administration (FDA) allows manufacturers to make claims on food labels about oats' ability to reduce risk of heart disease. You may have seen the claim "Soluble fiber from oatmeal, as part of a diet low in saturated fat and cholesterol, may reduce the risk of heart disease." Three grams of soluble fiber from whole oats daily is needed for the cholesterol-lowering effect, and to make this claim, an oatmeal product must contain at least 0.75 gram of soluble fiber per serving, according to the FDA. Keep in mind that the amount of soluble fiber varies—old-fashioned and quick-cooking oatmeal typically have 2 grams of soluble fiber per serving. Instant oatmeal typically contains 1 gram. There are exceptions, however, so be sure to read food labels to see how much soluble fiber you're getting.

Oatmeal is rich in B vitamins. Eating a serving of oatmeal in the morning helps to give you an energizing start to your day. If you have high cholesterol, I recommend eating oatmeal for breakfast as often as possible, and the more soluble fiber from oats, the better.

Sweet Spot on Sugar

Flavored instant oatmeal can contain anywhere from 12 grams to 16 grams of sugar per packet. Old-fashioned rolled oats contain about 1 gram of sugar per serving. If you want a sweet taste but don't want excess sugar, choose an oatmeal that's low in sugar (1 or 2 grams); then add a teaspoon of sugar, or a noncaloric sweetener, such as Splenda, and top it with berries. (You can find low-sugar oatmeal already made with Splenda, which cuts the sugar in half and brings the calories down to 110, versus 160 for the full-sugar version.)

Newer oatmeals on store shelves offer other heart-protective nutrients in addition to soluble fiber. Quaker's Take Heart, for instance, is marketed to help lower high blood pressure. It is lower in sodium than other instant oatmeals and contains B vitamins and potassium, which is beneficial for people with hypertension and heart disease. Kashi's Heart to Heart also contains potassium and is low in sodium. It's a bit higher in sugars (13 grams or 16 grams, versus 9 grams) but contains the same amount of B vitamins and antioxidants as Take Heart.

3. Fatty Fish

Fatty fish such as salmon, mackerel, and trout are excellent sources of omega-3 fatty acids (specifically, docoasahexaenoic acid and eicosapentaenoic acid), which help to decrease heart disease risk by lowering cholesterol and triglycerides, a type of blood fat. These omega-3s also prevent blood clots and decrease risk of arrhythmias, which can lead to sudden cardiac death. If you're concerned about heart disease and stroke, I recommend consuming fish three times per week. If you're pregnant or planning on becoming pregnant, however, avoid high-mercury fish, including king mackerel, tilefish, shark, swordfish, and "ahi" (big eye) tuna. Also, limit albacore tuna to six ounces per week. Instead, go for fish and shellfish that are low in mercury such as shrimp, herring, salmon, sole, tilapia, cod, crab, scallops, flounder, and catfish.

4. Soy Foods

Studies have shown that soy protein, which is present in tofu, tempeh, and soy-based meat alternatives, can lower LDL cholesterol levels. Specifically, 25 grams of soy protein per day can reduce high LDL cholesterol levels by about 10 percent, according to a current food claim approved by the FDA. It's thought that estrogen-like compounds called isoflavones play a role in soy's cholesterol-lowering effects. While recent research has revealed conflicting results on soy and heart disease, there's no good reason not to include soy foods in your diet, especially because they offer fiber, B vitamins, iron, and polyunsaturated fats. Incorporate whole soy foods into your diet, such as soy milk, tofu, edamame, and soy burgers, which offer very little saturated fat, compared to hamburgers.

5. Tomatoes

Tomatoes may offer us cardiovascular benefits. According to research from the Women's Health Initiative Study, an ongoing clinical trial involving more than 39,000 women, those who consumed the most tomato sauce and pizza (at least two servings per week of each) had a reduction in cardiovascular disease risk. Specifically, women who consumed at least seven tomato-based products per week had a 30 percent reduction in cardiovascular disease risk, compared with women consuming less than one and a half servings per week. It's thought that lycopene, an antioxidant, and perhaps other phytochemicals in tomatoes play a role in reducing risk, especially when tomatoes are cooked or consumed with oil. This diet includes plenty of tomatoes (with vinaigrette dressings) as part of your sandwiches and salads—and, of course, pizza options as well!

Focus on Fats

Have you ever tried to limit your consumption of fat grams in order to lose weight? I can certainly remember when a few of my friends were fat-phobic and declared a zero-tolerance policy for fat, especially when trying to shed pounds. The truth is that fats can be either friends or foes, depending on the type. This applies especially to the role of fat in protection against heart disease. Although low-fat diets have been recommended for heart health in the past, including more healthful fats in your diet can actually provide heart-protective benefits. In one recent Penn State study, a moderate-fat weight-loss diet comprising heart-healthy fats reduced dieters' cardiovascular risk *better* than a low-fat diet! The moderate-fat diet, in which half the fat was monounsaturated fat from peanuts and peanut oil, produced a 14 percent reduction in cardiovascular disease risk. The low-fat group experienced a 9 percent improvement. Weight loss was about the same in both groups.

Good Fats, Bad Fats

If I told you an egg a day is OK, but you are better off without butter, you may be puzzled. The advice makes sense once you understand the types of fat in these foods and their impact on your health. Butter contains saturated fats, which increase cholesterol levels in the bloodstream to a greater extent than dietary cholesterol. Specifically, saturated fats increase LDL, the harmful type of cholesterol. Even though an egg contains more than two-thirds of your daily limit for cholesterol, the cholesterol's impact in the bloodstream isn't as great as that of saturated fat when it comes to heart health. Aside from butter, sources of saturated fats include lard, cream, full-fat dairy products, red meat, palm oil, and coconut oil. You won't find many of these foods in this plan because it's best to limit them as much as possible.

Trans fats, formed when vegetable oils undergo a process known as hydrogenation, also increase LDL and risk of heart disease; moreover, they decrease HDL (high-density lipoprotein)—the good kind of cholesterol. Recently, the Institute of Medicine concluded that no amount of trans fat in the diet is safe. Trans fats are contained in hard margarines, french fries and other deep-fried foods such as doughnuts, and commercially prepared foods such as cookies and cakes. (Small amounts of trans fat exist naturally in meat and dairy foods, but these trans don't pose the risk that other sources of trans do.) As of January 2006, food manufacturers are required by the FDA to list trans fats on nutrition labels, underneath the total fat content. To spot trans, you can also look for the words *partially hydrogenated vegetable oil*, *hydrogenated oil*, or *shortening* in the ingredient list. If these words are listed as one of the first few ingredients, and the food is high in total fat, then you can assume the food is high in trans fats.

On the other hand, monounsaturated fats, which constitute much of the fat in the heart-healthy Mediterranean-style diet, decrease LDL levels, without lowering HDL. Sources of monounsaturated fats include almonds, walnuts, peanuts, macadamia nuts, avocados, peanut butter, olives, and olive and canola oils.

As you know, omega-3 fatty acids, which are a type of polyunsaturated fat, also have heart-protective properties. Their effects on the body include lowering LDL cholesterol and triglycerides, preventing blood clots, and reducing inflammation in blood vessels, thereby decreasing the chance of a heart attack or stroke. Sources of omega-3s include fatty fish, such as salmon, trout, mackerel, and herring. Flaxseeds and walnuts also contain omega-3 fats; however, the longer-chained omega-3 fats found in fish seem to offer greater heart-protective benefits. Other polyunsaturated fats, known as omega-6 fats, are found in vegetable oils, such as sunflower, safflower, and corn oil. These fats also help to lower LDL cholesterol.

Bottom line? Fats such as omega-3 fats in fish, as well as monounsaturated fats in nuts, olive oil, and canola oil, can protect your heart, whereas saturated fats and trans fats increase your risk of heart disease. Because fat is calorie dense, you need to monitor portion sizes of high-fat foods. This plan takes all these factors into account, providing you with a healthy dose of heart-protective fats, with minimal amounts of harmful fats.

Guide to Good Fats, Bad Fats

Include
- Monounsaturated fats, found in nuts, olives, avocados, peanut butter, and olive and canola oils
- Polyunsaturated fats, especially omega-3 fats found in omega-3 eggs and fatty fish including salmon, herring, and trout

Limit
- Saturated fats, found in high-fat dairy foods, red and processed meats, butter, palm, and coconut oils
- Trans fats, found in hard margarines, french fries, and commercially prepared baked goods, including high-fat cakes, cookies, and doughnuts
- Total cholesterol to 300 mg/day, or 200 mg if you have high LDL cholesterol (above 130 mg per deciliter). One large egg contains 213 mg of cholesterol.

Focus on High Blood Pressure

Extensive research into the effects of diet on cardiovascular risk confirms that fruits, vegetables, and low-fat dairy foods are major players in lowering high blood pressure. One particular study, known as DASH-Sodium (Dietary Approaches to Stop Hypertension), demonstrated that individuals following a heart-healthy diet rich in these foods, with limited amounts of sodium, experienced sig-

Code Words for Sodium

You won't necessarily see the words *sodium* or *salt* when trying to spot sodium on food labels. Here are code words for sodium you're likely to see:

Na (the scientific symbol for sodium)
MSG
Baking soda
Baking powder
Brine
Soy sauce
Teriyaki sauce

nificant blood pressure benefits. The study followed two groups: one consumed a diet incorporating lots of fruits, vegetables, and low-fat dairy foods, while limiting red meat, sweets, and saturated fats—the DASH diet. Another group was given a "typical" American diet. Different sodium levels, including 3,300 mg, 2,400 mg, and 1,500 mg, were prescribed every four weeks. When individuals followed the DASH diet and limited sodium to 1,500 mg/day, or about two-thirds of a teaspoon of salt, they registered the greatest reductions in blood pressure among all participants. For both diets, however, the greater the reduction in sodium, the lower the individuals' blood pressure readings.

Not everyone is "sodium sensitive"—that is, likely to experience an increase in blood pressure with high sodium intakes and a decrease in blood pressure with reduced sodium intakes. Regardless, it won't hurt to cut back on salt. New dietary guidelines recommend limiting your intake to less than 2,300 mg of sodium per day. Keep in mind that most of the sodium in your diet comes from processed food—such as canned soups and sauces, cured meats, and fast foods. On the other hand, potassium-rich foods such as bananas, oranges, and potatoes can help prevent or lower high blood pressure, by keeping sodium levels in check.

I'm filling you in on the DASH research because the components of the diet are similar to The 30s Health Prescription. In addition to offering blood pressure benefits, the diet has been shown to lower cholesterol and homocysteine levels (high blood levels of both have been linked to heart disease).

Spotlight on Snacking

Snacks are an integral component of this plan. In addition to their metabolism-elevating benefits, eating smaller meals more frequently throughout the day can positively affect cholesterol levels, thereby

Are You Prehypertensive?

New blood pressure guidelines were recently issued in the *Seventh Report of the Joint National Committee on Prevention, Detection, Evaluation, and Treatment of High Blood Pressure (JNC VII)*. Under these stricter guidelines, a resting blood pressure reading *below* 120/80 millimeters of mercury (mm Hg) is now considered a normal reading.

In other words, 120/80 is no longer the target for optimal blood pressure. Researchers now say a reading of 115/75 is the level above which your risk of cardiovascular complications starts to increase.

If your resting blood pressure is consistently 140/90 mm Hg or higher, you have high blood pressure. A reading in between these levels places you in the "prehypertensive" category.

Blood Pressure Classification

High blood pressure	140/90
Prehypertensive	120/80–139/89
Normal	below 120/80

Sources: National Heart, Lung, and Blood Institute; JNC VII

reducing the risk of heart disease. A recent study published in the *British Medical Journal* found that individuals who ate six or more small meals a day had lower cholesterol levels than those who ate one or two large meals. This supports earlier research published in the *New England Journal of Medicine*, which found that a "nibbling" diet, in which individuals consumed 17 snacks per day, resulted in lowered total and LDL cholesterol levels, compared with a "gorging" diet, in which subjects consumed only three meals per day. Both "nibbling" and "gorging" diets were equal in total calories.

Chocolate for Your Heart

The good word is that chocolate may be good for you. It contains antioxidants known as catechins, and these substances may help to reduce heart disease risk by decreasing the harmful effects of LDL cholesterol. Specifically, these antioxidants help to prevent the oxidation of LDL particles, and that helps to reduce the risk of heart attack and stroke.

A study published in the *Journal of the American Dietetic Association* included the intriguing finding that the catechin content of chocolate is four times greater than that of tea! Based on the study, dark chocolate is the best in this respect. It has the highest total catechin content, with 53.5 mg per 100 grams; milk chocolate contained 15.9 mg per 100 grams, while black tea contained only 13.9 mg per 100 milliliter. Cocoa powder is the source of chocolate's catechins (also known as flavonoids), and because dark chocolate contains the most cocoa powder (white chocolate doesn't have any), it also contains the highest amount of catechins, compared with milk chocolate and white chocolate. (Note: If the label on chocolate says "Dutch processed" with alkali, it means that flavonoids have been removed).

A third of the fat in cocoa butter comprises stearic acid, a type of saturated fat. In addition to chocolate's antioxidant benefits, research suggests that unlike other saturated fats, the stearic acid in chocolate doesn't seem to increase LDL cholesterol—it appears to have a neutral effect.

Before you run for your chocolate fix, remember that chocolate counts as a "C" snack on this plan. Eating too much of it will increase calories and pounds, outweighing any possible heart benefits!

Amanda's Story

Amanda, a successful media buying exec, knew how to climb the corporate ladder. Well-liked and respected, she had secured several media placements for her company and was rewarded with more challenging roles and responsibilities each year. But as Amanda's position got bigger, so did her clothing size. When we first met, she weighed 296.5 pounds. A single, otherwise healthy, exuberant blond eager to find the love of her life, Amanda was desperate to lose weight.

When I first looked at Amanda's food records, I couldn't identify any calorie culprits. But when I asked her whether or not she ate in response to boredom, stress, or depression, her answer was "Yes." Amanda then revealed that her huge demands at work and her on-again, off-again relationship with her boyfriend would put her in a funk, and she would seek large portions of sweets. Her choice of sweets depended on the season or occasion. When Easter came, she would load up on bags of mini Cadbury eggs. During observance of Passover, she stocked her apartment weeks in advance with macaroons and chocolate-covered marshmallow twists to make sure she would have treats on demand. To cope with birthday blues, Amanda chose to indulge herself with an ice-cream sundae and candy. Amanda even told me how she and her friend would go to the Comfort Diner in New York, when they were experiencing low moods to vent over grilled cheese sandwiches and large chocolate milkshakes. Just about every time Amanda got upset or stressed, she would soothe herself with large portions of sugary or fatty foods. As a result, she gained a significant amount of weight in a short period of time.

I described The 30s Health Prescription to Amanda and explained that it was important not to deny herself sweets (which she admitted wouldn't be feasible), but rather to keep her portions limited to those on the "C" snack list. While difficult at first, Amanda got into her daily diet groove and looked forward to a preportioned "C" snack each evening. To make it a bit easier and less tempting, Amanda limited herself to prepackaged snacks such as low-fat ice-cream pops and avoided bringing boxes of sweets into her home. This strategy made the plan doable for Amanda, and after five months, she lost 25 pounds!

Amanda laughs when she describes her experience on The 30s Health Prescription. "I tell my friends that I can eat whatever I want, and they look at me funny. But deep down, I know I can, as long as I limit my portions."

Protection Against Cancer

As you reach your 30s, your risk for cancer, a disease of aging, increases. As with other diseases, keeping weight in check can go far to lower cancer risk. Being overweight or obese is associated with an increased risk for developing cancers of the breast (among postmenopausal women), colon, endometrium, gallbladder, esophagus, pancreas, kidney, and possibly other sites. Other factors that increase cancer risk, aside from genetics, include eating foods high in animal fat, such as red and other processed meats; smoking; and ingesting too many carcinogens—harmful chemicals from foods or the environment that can initiate cancer in your body.

According to the American Institute for Cancer Research (AICR), 30 percent to 40 percent of all cancers could be prevented by eating a healthful diet, being physically active, and maintaining a healthy body weight. For your diet, this implies consuming lots of fruits, vegetables, and other plant-based foods such as whole grains; avoiding foods high in saturated fat and salt; limiting red and processed meats; and drinking alcohol only in moderation.

Cancer-Fighting Fare: Fruits, Vegetables, and Foods Rich in Antioxidants

One of the cornerstones of cancer prevention is eating a wide variety of fruits and vegetables. In a comprehensive report on nutrition and cancer, the AICR estimated that cancer rates could drop by at least 20 percent if the only change we made was to eat at least five servings of fruits and vegetables each day. In fact, the National Cancer Institute recommends aiming for "nine a day" (and new dietary guidelines have followed in those footsteps), instead of the previously popular "five a day," to maximize protection. Additionally, many epidemiological studies have found

Top 20 Antioxidant-Rich Foods

Antioxidants act as cancer weapons by ridding the body of harmful chemicals that cause cell damage, which can lead to the development of cancer. While antioxidants have not been studied extensively in humans, scientists are learning more and more about how they work in the body and about which ones (especially phytochemicals) may affect specific cancers.

You can be confident in getting your daily dose of antioxidants from your "A" snacks and vegetables. Still, you may be wondering which foods give you the *biggest* nutritional bang for your bite. There's no need to guess—we now have a "Top 20" list of antioxidant-rich foods, compiled by USDA researchers. Your antiaging breakfasts and "A" snacks incorporate fruits from this list—particularly raspberries, blueberries, and strawberries.

Best Sources of Food Antioxidants

RANK	FOOD ITEM	SERVING SIZE
1	Small red bean (dried)*	Half cup
2	Wild blueberry**	1 cup
3	Red kidney bean (dried)*	Half cup
4	Pinto bean (dried)*	Half cup
5	Cultivated blueberry**	1 cup
6	Cranberry	1 cup
7	Artichoke	1 cup (hearts)
8	Blackberry	1 cup
9	Prune	Half cup
10	Raspberry	1 cup
11	Strawberry	1 cup
12	Red Delicious apple	One
13	Granny Smith apple	One
14	Pecan	1 ounce
15	Sweet cherry	1 cup
16	Black plum	One
17	Russet potato	One
18	Black bean (dried)*	Half cup
19	Plum	One
20	Gala apple	One

*A half cup of dried beans would translate to about 1 cup cooked. While cooking the beans might decrease the amount of antioxidants present, the beans would still be a good source of these flavonoids (specifically proanthocyanins), because the levels in dried beans are so high.

**Cultivated blueberries are not as sweet as the wild type.

Source: Journal of Agricultural and Food Chemistry

associations between high fruit and vegetable consumption and decreased cancer risk among individuals.

What's in fruits and vegetables that make them nutritional powerhouses? They contain natural chemicals known as phytochemicals that have antioxidant properties—meaning that they are capable of warding off carcinogens in your body known as free radicals. Free radicals are oxygen molecules that cause DNA damage to cells, and it's the cell damage that can lead to mutations and ultimately cancer.

On this plan, your phytochemical intake comes from your "A" snacks, your fruits at breakfast, and your lunch and dinner plates that consist of one-third vegetables and one-third grains. If you have a family history of cancer, I recommend consuming plant-based proteins (for example, tofu and hummus) at least twice per week.

Cancer Concern: Farmed Salmon

If you're concerned about the safety of salmon, you're not

alone. A recent study reported higher levels of environmental contaminants, including PCBs (polychlorinated biphenyls), in farmed salmon than in wild salmon. PCBs are present in the food on which farmed fish feed and have been shown to cause cancer and other health problems in animals.

Despite these facts, there's no need to throw salmon out of your diet—even the farmed kind. The study showed that some of the lowest levels of PCBs were found in farmed salmon from North and South America. Given that more than 90 percent of the farmed salmon consumed in the United States is from the Americas, and the PCB levels detected in the study are not believed to present a public health concern, the FDA advises consumers not to alter their consumption of farmed or wild salmon.

If you're still concerned about contaminants in salmon, you can reduce the number of PCBs by removing the skin and the fat under the fish before you cook it. Then instead of sautéing the fish in oil, broil or poach it. This can reduce the PCBs, as the fish store them in fat. You can also trim any visible fat from fish to reduce PCBs.

Cancer Concern: Red and Processed Meats

You'll find that red and processed meats are rare on this plan. Although red meat is an excellent source of heme iron, regular consumption has been associated with increased risk for colorectal cancer. One recent study from the American Cancer Society involving more than 150,000 adults found that those who consumed a high intake of red and processed meat had a 30 percent to 50 percent higher risk of colorectal cancer than those who consumed little or no red or processed meat. "High" was defined for women as eating at least two ounces of red meat *each day*. Red meat included beef, pork, lamb, and hamburger. For processed meat, high intake was defined for women as eating one ounce two to three days per week. Processed meat included bacon, hot dogs, lunchmeat, and sausages.

The increased risk could be due to the saturated fat content in red and processed meats—previous research has suggested this. Also, processed meats contain nitrates, which are chemicals that may get converted to carcinogens in the body. Another theory is that cooking red meat at very high temperatures when grilling or frying can cause the formation of carcinogens known as heterocyclic amines; if these carcinogens get ingested, the cancer risk can increase. (These chemicals have been shown to cause cancer in animals.) Bottom line? Limit your consumption of red meat to no more than once per week, and avoid all processed meats.

Focus on Breast Cancer

According to the American Cancer Society, excluding cancers of the skin, breast cancer is the most common cancer among women, accounting for nearly one in three cancers diagnosed in American women. While risk factors such as family history are beyond your control, there are several risk factors that you *can* control to help to protect yourself from the disease.

Lifestyle Tips for Breast Cancer Prevention

By following The 30s Health Prescription, you are inherently protecting yourself from disease, including breast cancer. I want to outline some tips in detail based on the latest breast cancer research.

Staying slim during your younger years can help to ward off breast cancer. By the time you reach menopause, if you've gained enough weight to be considered obese, you have one and a half times the risk of breast cancer compared with a woman of normal weight. The increased risk is thought to be due to increased levels of estrogen in overweight postmenopausal women. Estrogen is produced in fat tissue as well as the ovaries; after menopause, when the ovaries stop producing hormones, fat cells are called on for estrogen. So, the theory is that the more fat cells you have, the more estrogen is produced, and the higher the risk becomes. The risk seems to increase with a body mass index (BMI) of 25 or above (weighing 150 pounds at 5′4″ is associated with a BMI of 26).

On the flip side, one recent study published in *Breast Cancer Research* found that younger women at high risk for breast cancer experience reduced risk with weight loss. Specifically, women carrying the BRCA1 gene mutation (a high-risk group) who lost 10 pounds had a 65 percent reduced risk of the disease, compared with women who didn't lose or gain 10 pounds. For this high-risk group, researchers caution that weight gain should be avoided between the ages of 18 and 30.

Avoid More than One Alcoholic Beverage a Day

Consuming alcohol is a risk factor for developing breast cancer. According to the American Cancer Society's *Breast Cancer Facts and Figures 2005–2006*, a meta-analysis that included more than 40 epidemiological studies, the equivalent of two drinks per day—or 24 grams of alcohol—may increase breast cancer risk by 21 percent. Alcohol also increases the risk of cancers of the mouth, pharynx, larynx, esophagus, and liver.

I recommend limiting alcohol consumption to no more than three drinks per week. One drink is 5 ounces of wine, 12 ounces of beer, or 1.5 ounces of 80-proof liquor. Also, make sure you are meeting your folic acid requirements (400 micrograms), because folic acid may provide some protection against the disease among those who consume alcohol. A recent study in the *British Medical Journal* found that women with a high consumption of alcohol (about three alcoholic beverages a day) and a low intake of folate had an increased risk of breast cancer, compared with those with higher folate intakes. If you have a family history of breast cancer, avoid alcohol as much as possible.

Exercise Away Your Risk

A recent study in the *Journal of the American Medical Association* showed that women who engaged in the equivalent of one and a quarter to two and a half hours per week of brisk walking (about 20 minutes a day, based on the upper limit) had an 18 percent decreased risk of breast cancer, compared with inactive women. According to Dr. Ahmedin Jemal, author of the American Cancer Society's *Breast Cancer Facts and Figures 2005–2006*, many epidemiological studies reveal a positive association between exercise and reduced risk for the disease.

Soy and Breast Cancer

If you eat foods rich in soy protein, can you reduce your breast cancer risk? It's hard to say at this time. We know that Asian women eat soy on a daily basis and have lower rates of breast cancer, but it's difficult to determine if soy is the protective factor. The increased protection may be due to the fact that Asian women consume fewer calories and saturated fat, for example.

According to a recent study in the *Journal of the American Dietetic Association*, research is attempting to find whether soy has a role in the prevention or treatment of chronic diseases, including breast cancer, but right now, the data are inconclusive.

Exercise appears to reduce estrogen levels. This may be owing to the fact that women who exercise have less body fat, which becomes the main source of estrogen after menopause.

Limit Red Meat and High-Fat Dairy, but Include Cruciferous Vegetables

While there is no *conclusive* evidence that limiting red meat and high-fat dairy will decrease breast cancer risk, there is no good reason not to accept this diet advice. The same logic applies for eating more cruciferous vegetables, such as broccoli, cauliflower, and cabbage. These vegetables contain phytochemicals that may offer cancer protection by reducing cell damage that can lead to cancer. While we can't say that eating them will necessarily prevent disease, we can say that including them in our diet can help to stack the odds in our favor.

Now that you know how to keep your body healthy, it's time to put the plan into practice. Get ready for a slimmer, healthier, more beautiful you!

PART 2

The 30s Health Prescription

The Plan

et psyched! It's time to treat yourself to a nutritious, balanced, antiaging plan that will keep you beautiful and slim for years to come. This is a plan that is totally specific to *your* health, beauty, and lifestyle needs. I'm going to show you how easy it is to nourish your body and mind with delicious meals and snacks that will keep your health, weight, and appearance in its best shape ever.

When designing The 30s Health Prescription, I took great care to ensure that the plan addressed many of the nutritional and lifestyle issues 30-something women are faced with. I didn't want to bore you with a generic diet plan that you could find in ten other different, slightly altered versions. I was instead inspired to give you something unique for you— a plan that is a bit more sophisticated and chic and that takes into account your unique physical and lifestyle needs.

With this concept in mind, I created a plan to help you rid yourself of extra body fat, nourish your hair and skin, ward off age-related diseases, and boost fertility. When I designed your meal and snack combinations, I made sure they were packed with antiaging, bone-building, and metabolism-boosting nutrients. You can rest assured that The 30s Health Prescription will keep you looking and feeling great at all times.

Additionally, I wanted to make sure that my meal and snack suggestions would be appealing to you. Because our palates may prefer different foods, you have a range of combinations to choose from, including Chinese, Greek, Mexican, Japanese, Italian, and vegetarian dishes. I also wanted to ensure that your meals and snacks consisted of practical, realistic fare, no matter what your day-to-day life entails. After all, you need an eating plan that fits into your busy schedule. So, whether you are in the midst of a hectic workweek, a crazy mommy-and-me schedule, or a much needed getaway to St. Bart's, you have tempting options—from homemade dishes and smoothies to frozen meals and energy bars. And if you don't like one combination, there's no need to stress—you can choose a different one, or you can scan the list of substitutions I've provided for you. You can even have a meal or snack that doesn't appear on the plan, as long as you stick to the specific calorie and nutrient guidelines for your meals and snacks, which I include in each meal plan. You can simply gear your selections to these to ensure that you're staying on track.

The 30s Health Prescription Nutrient Guidelines

The 30s Health Prescription is a calorie-controlled plan that is moderate in carbohydrates and protein, low in fat, and filled with antiaging foods! Here's a glimpse of its major characteristics:

- It's calorie controlled for weight loss—you'll first choose either the 1,200-, 1,400-, or 1,600-calorie plan.
- It's moderate in protein to preserve muscle mass, boost metabolism, and curb cravings. Protein makes up 20 percent to 30 percent of your total calorie intake.

- It's rich in whole grains and fiber while providing a moderate amount of carbohydrates—specifically, 50 percent of your total calories is from carbohydrates.
- It's low in fat, with fat constituting 20 percent to 30 percent of total calories. These are mostly healthful fats, including monounsaturated and polyunsaturated fats, with a minimal amount of saturated and trans fats.
- It's loaded with antioxidant-rich foods, to maximize antiaging nutrients for protection against diseases including heart disease and cancer.
- It's rich in bone-building foods and meets daily calcium needs of 1,000 milligrams (mg).
- It contains ample amounts of vitamins and minerals to provide nourishment for youthful, glowing skin and shiny, healthy-looking hair.
- It doesn't require giving up your favorite foods! Comfort foods, including sweets and chocolate, are incorporated into your plan!

Begin with Breakfast, and Then Picture Your Plate in Thirds

Here's your basic meal strategy on the plan: Start your day off with an antiaging breakfast and then, for lunches and dinners, visualize your plate consisting of three meal components: protein, vegetables, and grains.

Antiaging Breakfast

Your breakfast is filled with antiaging nutrients that will help you shed pounds while staying healthy and youthful. Each breakfast includes a source of whole grains or fiber, which will slowly elevate your blood sugar (glucose) in the morning, providing you with sustained energy until the afternoon. Your breakfasts are also moderate in protein, to boost metabolism, increase alertness, and prevent late-morning cravings. These meals contain prime antioxidant-rich fruits, to optimize your intake of antiaging nutrients. Each breakfast also includes a bone-building food, with a quarter of your daily calcium needs.

The combination of protein with fiber and whole grains in your breakfasts gives you the optimal source of fuel to get each day started. The vitamins, minerals, and antioxidants in your breakfasts, including B vitamins, vitamins A and C, calcium, and several polyphenols in fruits, offer essential nutrition for your overall health and metabolism. Note: While your breakfasts do contain sources of folate, if pregnancy is in your near-future plans, aim to include cereals fortified with folic acid (the synthetic form of the vitamin).

Lunches and Dinners

Your lunches and dinners were created to ensure that you are getting an adequate amount of protein for your metabolism and weight-loss needs; a variety of vegetables for your antiaging needs; and grains for energy, including whole grains for overall health. As a visual guide, you can picture your plate in thirds for lunches and dinners—one-third each of protein, vegetables, and grains. Your protein source will ensure that you are maintaining muscle mass, which allows your metabolism to function at full speed during weight loss. This is especially important when you're attempting to shed pounds. The protein in your meals will also keep you satiated and prevent you from craving sweets and other snacks. Fish, especially fatty fish such as salmon, is an excellent source of protein and omega-3 fatty acids—heart-protective fats that also keep your skin looking smooth and radiant. Because of all of the health benefits associated with fish, I recommend consuming fish three times per week.

Similar to the design for your breakfasts, whole grains are the preferred source of starchy carbohydrates for lunch and dinner, because they provide fiber and are filled with important B vitamins. Whole grains are also associated with protection against obesity, heart disease, diabetes, and possibly cancer. One point I want to make clear: Don't feel that you're going "off" the plan if you don't have whole grains at *every* meal. In fact, you may wish to aim for whole grains at either lunch *or* dinner. The more whole grains, the better, but they don't have to be your only source of starchy carbohydrates.

Your vegetables will provide you with a low-calorie source of vitamins, antioxidants, and fiber. Here's where a lot of your antiaging nutrients come into play. Remember, if you don't love a vegetable you see, you can simply replace it with one you enjoy. Keep in mind, though, that corn and peas are OK mixed in with a starch or vegetable (in a salad, or with orzo, for example), but by themselves, they count as starchy carbohydrates. The reason is that they have more calories (due to their higher carbohydrate counts) than vegetables such as carrots, broccoli, and spinach.

Remember, if you don't feel like having the exact meal or snack as described, you can choose an alternative from the substitution lists in Appendix A. This plan is all about flexibility, so there's no need to conform to every detail exactly as it appears. As long as you adhere to the appropriate calorie and nutrient guidelines, you will not sabotage your efforts one bit.

Add Your "ABC's" as Snacks

Snacks are a key component of this plan. By eating small snacks, you keep your metabolism running at full speed and avoid overeating at meals. While this is especially important when you're trying to lose extra pounds, or simply keep your weight in check, snacking pays dividends beyond weight control. Munching or sipping nutritious snacks gives your brain energy and enables you to concentrate better on difficult tasks that require deep thought. Additionally, carbohydrate-rich snacks give muscles the fuel they need for exercise.

You'll find separate lists of antiaging ("A") snacks, bone-building ("B") snacks, and comfort ("C") snacks. Aim to have your snacks between meals, three to four hours apart. That schedule will help to keep your blood sugar from going too high or too low and will give you an energy boost when it's most needed.

Antiaging ("A") Snacks

Your "A" snacks include fruits that offer antiaging nutrients for your skin, such as beta-carotene and vitamin C, as well as B vitamins, such as vitamin B_6 and folic acid, which are essential for healthy hair. Dried apricots and cantaloupe are two good sources of beta-carotene and vitamin C; bananas and watermelon are rich in B vitamins. Your list of antiaging snacks also incorporates fruits from the top 20 antioxidant-rich foods, as compiled by the United States Department of Agriculture. These antioxidants help to rid the body of harmful free radicals that may contribute to heart disease and cancer, among other diseases.

The fruits in your "A" snacks are accompanied by small portions of nuts, such as almonds, pecans, and walnuts, because the protein and healthful fats in them will keep you more satiated than would eating fruit alone. When you eat fruit by itself (especially dried fruit), you are consuming a concentrated source of carbohydrates, which rapidly floods your bloodstream with sugar. Combining some fat or protein with a carbohydrate-rich food allows blood sugar to increase at a slower rate, which in turn allows you to feel satisfied longer. Another asset is that nuts contain vitamin E, which helps to maintain smooth, healthy skin.

Bone-Building ("B") Snacks

Your bone-building ("B") snacks include a quarter of your daily calcium needs (250 mg) and at least five grams of protein. These bone-building snacks are also low in saturated fat, the fat that raises levels of LDL (low-density lipoprotein)—the harmful cholesterol. I've given you delicious dairy options to choose from, as well as calcium-fortified foods, so you have free range depending on your taste preferences.

If you find that you're having trouble getting your "B" snacks in, I recommend taking a calcium supplement (at least 500 mg) and substituting your "B" calories with an "A" snack. (Of course, sometimes the extra calories may go toward a "C" snack—for example, if you're at a party and eat twice the amount of cookies you had planned on.) Meeting your calcium needs is important for keeping your bones strong, and if you can't do it through foods, a supplement is your next line of defense. I prefer aiming for foods first, especially because dairy foods contain lots of other nutrients that are important for your health. A recent study published in the *Journal of the American Dietetic Association* found that intakes of several vitamins and minerals—including calcium, magnesium, potassium, zinc, folate, thiamin, riboflavin, and vitamins B_6, B_{12}, A, D, and E—were higher when individuals consumed a greater number of dairy servings. If you choose a calcium supplement, check to see that it contains 100 to 200 international units (IU) of vitamin D, for better absorption of the mineral.

Comfort ("C") Snacks

Your comfort ("C") snacks include some sweet and some salty "indulgent" snacks—such as pretzels, chips, chocolate, and licorice. All of your "C" snacks are portioned and calorie controlled. When you indulge in a "C" snack on a daily basis, you won't feel deprived of your favorite treats, even when you are losing weight!

You can consume your three types of snacks in any order you like, as long as they are spaced out between meals. However, I recommend saving your "C" snack for after dinner. If you tend to have cravings at work or when you're running around during the day, you will be better off having an "A" or "B" snack, because they contain more protein than

"C" snacks. In other words, "A" and "B" snacks will go further in helping you curb cravings than "C" snacks will. Plus, you may be less likely to overconsume "C" snacks if they are last on your to-eat list.

Natalie's Story

For Natalie, a San Francisco marketing professional, being in shape was never a challenge. "I used to work out all the time," says Natalie, who says she moved to San Francisco partly to seek out a healthier lifestyle. "When I moved here, I did two marathons."

Now this 32-year-old's lifestyle is less marathons and more Mallomars. With a demanding career, a new husband, and ever-increasing social and personal obligations, Natalie's healthy lifestyle caved in to the demands of true adulthood. Before long, just as she was settling into her career and marriage, the pounds started to settle in as well. Twenty of them to be exact.

Natalie's lifestyle wasn't exactly a dieter's dream. One of her greatest saboteurs was lunchtime, when getting out of the office was a stress release or office social event. "We go as a group to burrito shops like Baja Fresh, where I order a burrito that I can almost eat in its entirety." Natalie realized that if she left the office for lunch, she was in a diet danger zone. But Natalie also found that she was back in the danger zone whenever the stress level was turned up. She found herself frequently nibbling, grabbing a piece of chocolate or some other comfort food to distract herself. "I have been stressed a lot in this past year, and hence, I have put on the pounds."

When I first introduced her to The 30s Health Prescription, Natalie had a very positive response to her choices. "The beauty of the plan is that it's real food. You're not banned from eating 'good food,'" says Natalie. Besides having the ability to make substitutions, the concept of "A," "B," and "C" snacks resonated with her. The variety and quantity of the snacks kept her from getting hungry and she found they were really easy to work into her daily habits.

Natalie and I came up with several strategies to avoid dieting pitfalls while on the plan. Because she knew that a lunch trip out of the office led to heavy calories and unhealthy fare, she brought back an old habit from grade school. She started brown-bagging it. A typical lunch went from a burrito to hummus on a whole wheat pita. She also started packing healthy "A" snacks the night before. She set aside Sundays for her grocery store shopping and meal planning for the workweek. One trick she found was that buying things she considered indulgent, like Hershey's Kisses and other "C" snacks, diminished her cravings.

All of her work and creative solutions have already paid off. Natalie has lost eight pounds since starting the plan! She's noticed that her clothes fit better and she's starting to see results in her belly, which really makes her happy because that's her "trouble zone." An added bonus is that her husband, Jamie, is eating healthier because of her, too.

More important, Natalie says she's happier because The 30s Health Prescription adds necessary structure to her daily routine. "I feel like I have more control over my harried and crazy life and definitely am getting more accomplished because I am not thinking about what I am going to eat at every juncture."

Determining Your Calorie Needs

When I determine a woman's calorie needs, I take several factors into account. I start by using clinical formulas that incorporate her weight, height, age, sex, and activity level. This gives me a ballpark figure of what amount she needs to consume in order to *maintain* her given weight. (The formulas are not 100 percent accurate.) I then subtract 500 calories for the person to *lose* one pound per week. This number is based on the fact that one pound is equivalent to 3,500 calories, so to lose one pound, you need a deficit of 500 calories each day (500 × 7 = 3,500 calories). If she plans to start an exercise regimen, I will subtract 300 calories, because on average, approximately 200 additional calories will be burned each day from physical activity. Of course, I also compare this number with the amount of calories she is currently consuming, to get a better idea of what the best calorie level would be for weight loss.

For example, if my formulas yield 1,200 calories for weight loss, but the person is used to consuming 2,000, I will start the person off a bit higher, perhaps at 1,400 or 1,600 calories. The idea is not only to figure out individual calorie needs based on clinical formulas, but also to compare these numbers against how much the person is currently consuming. Overall, this strategy helps me to prescribe a calorie level that will help people lose weight, while not taking them so low so that they feel extremely deprived.

Because I can't assess your needs individually, I'm going to give you some guidance based on the calorie categories applicable to most women I've counseled. Here's the deal: If you typically exercise three times per week or more, for at least 30 minutes, begin with the 1,600-calorie plan. This is a good starting point for most women. (If you find that you are hungry on 1,600 calories, you may add an extra "A," "B," or "C" snack.) If you typically exercise one or two times per week, or are planning to start exercising, begin with the 1,400-calorie plan.

The only circumstance in which I would prescribe 1,200 calories for you is if you have less than 10 pounds to lose and you don't plan on incorporating any formal exercise into your routine, at least in the early stages of your weight loss. Many women with whom I meet have not been exercising and are not consuming a significant excess of calories. They often like to start out by modifying their diet only—waiting until they get adjusted to their new eating habits before incorporating exercise. So, I may start them off with 1,200 calories and then transition them to 1,400 once they get into exercising. The only other time I may suggest 1,200 calories is if someone hits a prolonged plateau on 1,400 calories. Generally speaking, though, this level is not enough to sustain regular exercise.

Weekend Detox

By the time you enter start mode on The 30s Health Prescription, you may find you are supereager to get going on your pound-shedding journey. If that's the case (and for most women I've counseled, it is), I recommend a weekend detox— cutting out all starchy carbohydrates such as breads, crackers, pasta, rice, pretzels, cookies, and cakes. The reason is that carbohydrates are stored with water in your body. They get stored in the liver (as liver glycogen), and for every gram of carbohydrate, you store three grams of water. When you eliminate carbohydrates from your diet, you lose water, and the number on the scale goes down, even if you haven't been exercising. This is why you might have seen some of your friends lose up to seven pounds during the first week on a low-carbohydrate diet. True, all diets result in some water loss in the beginning, but eliminating carbohydrates produces the most drastic drop in water weight. Because the psychological impact can be pretty significant, and can be a necessary motivational "boost," I recommend incorporating this modified detox into your plan.

Beverages

As far as your beverage intake goes, I recommend aiming for eight glasses of water and tea combined per day. While caffeinated beverages may not be dehydrating as once thought, it's still advantageous to limit your caffeine intake to 300 mg per day (about two large cups of coffee, or three small). Too much caffeine can cause jitteriness and wreak havoc on blood sugar, leaving you craving carbohydrates. Tea—in particular, green tea—contains chemicals that may offer metabolism-boosting benefits, so I advocate drinking green tea as part of your total fluid intake.

Sometimes I'm asked if drinking water before a meal can help with weight loss. Drinking a glass of water before each meal may help you feel satisfied on fewer calories—as it may bloat you and make you feel less hungry before you eat—but technically speaking, drinking water without food satisfies only thirst, not hunger. So, the answer is yes, a glass of water before a meal may help you in your weight-loss efforts, but only if it helps you to eat less at your meal.

Vitamins

I tell all of my clients to take one multivitamin daily. It's a good idea generally because it supplies "nutritional insurance," and it's all the more important when following a calorie-restricted diet that may not include some of the foods you had previously been eating. Be assured that The 30s Health Prescription meets all of your nutrient needs, and if you're following it precisely, you should be satisfying all of your requirements. Still, it can't hurt to take a multivitamin, especially for the days when you may not be following the plan to a T.

Look for a multi that includes 100 percent of most vitamins and minerals, especially iron and folic acid. If you are skipping "B" snacks and other dairy foods, I recommend taking a calcium supplement with vitamin D. (See "Calcium Supplements" in Chapter 4). If you don't like to swallow large pills, Viactiv chews are a great option; each one provides 500 mg—or 50 percent—of your daily calcium needs and 25 percent of your D needs. You can also get Viactiv multivitamins in chewable form.

Exercise

To get the whole healthful package of a sexier body, higher energy level, boost in confidence, antiaging benefits, and an all-around healthier body, you absolutely must add exercise to the mix.

The merits of exercise—ranging from preventing chronic health conditions to boosting your confidence and self-esteem—are hard to ignore. But here's the real reason you bought this book: exercise burns calories. Your body requires a certain amount of energy to sustain life but, once you've fulfilled that need, the rest are just excess calories that get stored as—you guessed it—fat. Exercise allows you to burn more calories than you take in, enabling you to reduce body fat. Plus, as I addressed in Chapter 2, engaging in just 20 minutes of weight training twice a week will help you preserve muscle during weight loss. By strengthening your muscles, your metabolism can continue burning at an optimal rate.

The more intensely you exercise, the more calories you burn. One of the sheer beauties of exercise is that even after you stop exercising, your body continues to burn calories at a modestly increased rate for a few hours. Imagine that—your body continues to burn calories without your trying to—as long as you put in the initial investment.

If you don't like to engage in formal exercise, take a look at Appendix B, which contains a chart of the total calories burned by various physical activities.

Journaling

I highly recommend keeping a food journal. You don't have to share it with anyone; it's just for you and helps you to become accountable for everything you eat. When you know you're going to write down everything you put in your mouth, you may be less likely to give in to cravings for sweets, chips, alcohol, or whatever else it is that you desire.

Recent research supports the theory that journaling helps dieters lose weight and stick to their weight-loss plans. One study, published in *Health Psychology*, found that dieters who kept food records between Thanksgiving and New Year's continued to lose weight during the holiday period, whereas those who weren't as diligent during the holiday season ended up gaining back some of the weight they had previously lost. Additionally, research has shown that dieters who have successfully maintained their weight loss consistently monitor their progress, through journals and regular weigh-ins.

Weighing In

As with journaling, weighing yourself will help to keep you on track, giving you additional feedback on your progress. Your best approach for gauging your progress is to pick one day and time of the week to weigh yourself. I recommend stepping on the scale right after waking up in the morning, before you eat or drink anything. Being consistent with the timing of your weigh-ins will give you a more accurate picture of the amount of weight you're losing.

Bear in mind that it's normal for your weight to fluctuate from day to day, whether it's because you're eating at different times, or eating lots of salty foods (salt can cause water retention, and this can falsely raise the number on the scale), or because of other conditions. Drinking beverages can also cause a false weigh-in, due to increased water weight. Drinking just two cups of fluids can translate into one pound gained on the scale. Of course, there are days when the scale can read lower than what you really weigh. For example, alcoholic beverages can cause water loss, and this can affect the number on the scale. Because these minor day-to-day fluctuations do not necessarily represent true changes in body composition, I recommend sticking to a once-per-week weigh-in, for the most precise feedback on your progress.

Coping with Plateaus

At some point during your weight-loss journey, you may find that you're not losing weight as quickly as you were in the beginning. Many women start off losing one to two pounds per week and then find that their weight loss comes to a halt. If this happens, don't panic. You've simply hit a plateau, and it is a totally normal part of losing weight.

There are actually two types of weight-loss plateaus you can encounter. The first is what I call a miniplateau that occurs in the beginning stages of a diet—perhaps one to two weeks into your plan. You start to lose weight at a slower rate, because you are no longer losing a lot of water. As you now know, you can expect to lose fluids quickly when you begin a diet plan, but as you start to lose more body fat instead of water, the rate of weight loss slows down.

The second weight-loss plateau you may encounter occurs weeks or months after starting a diet, because as you lose weight, your body requires fewer calories to perform its daily functions, including breathing, circulation, and maintaining a normal body temperature. Recall from Chapter 2 that rate of metabolism is, in part, dependent on body size. The larger you are, the more calories you burn at rest. And the smaller you are, the fewer you burn. What this means is, when you hit a plateau, your body is telling you it's time to gradually cut back more calories, or increase the duration or intensity of your exercise, in order to continue losing weight.

Being prepared for the plateau will help you stay faithful to your plan and prevent you from being discouraged. If you hit it, start by increasing your exercise. You can boost either the amount of time you're exercising or the intensity of your workouts. For women who haven't been exercising, hitting a plateau is often the perfect opportunity to begin an exercise plan, because their eating habits are now under control.

If you find that increasing your exercise is not producing the results you want, try consuming 200 fewer calories each day. In other words, if you started on 1,600 calories, try the 1,400-calorie plan. If you started on 1,400 calories and have not been exercising, try the 1,200-calorie plan. (Note: 1,200 calories is usually too low when one is exercising regularly.) You will notice that the differences between the plans are not major; they are minor adjustments to portion sizes or the number of snacks.

If you started on 1,200 calories, however, I *do not* recommend cutting calories further—even if you have hit a plateau. Doing so will only slow your metabolism, and you will not have enough calories to meet your daily energy requirements. My advice at this point is to increase the amount or intensity of your physical activity—it is the only part of the equation you can change without compromising your health.

Now, time to get started on your plan. Choose the plan for which you think you are best suited, based on my advice. You will discover a whole new way of eating that will keep you healthy, slim, and strong for years to come!

The 1,200-Calorie Meal Plan

(6)

Your meal plans were designed with flexibility in mind. There are two general ways you can proceed: If you enjoy having the ability to choose what to eat each day, you can select meals and snacks from the respective lists in the first part of this chapter. You may find some offerings that you really like and decide to consume these more often than others. If, instead, you prefer more structure, you can turn to the chapter's complete two-week meal plan. Both formats contain the same components for meals and snacks. It's just a matter of which format works better for you.

Remember, the 1,200-calorie plan is an appropriate starting plan only if you have less than 10 pounds to lose and you are not currently engaging in any formal exercise. This is the lowest calorie level one should consume. If you find that you are uncomfortably hungry on this plan, or if you start incorporating exercise into your routine, I advise switching to the 1,400-calorie plan.

Please note that while brand names are often cited, they are *only* suggestions for what can be included on your plan. You can feel free to substitute other foods wherever you like, as long as the number of calories is the same. Also, see Appendix A for substitution lists.

Options Format

Your breakfasts comprise one serving of fruit (mostly the "antiaging" fruits, which are loaded with antioxidants) and one bone-building ("B") food. Each breakfast also contains a source of whole grains or other fiber-rich food and has a moderate amount of protein. Lunch and dinner plates can be visualized as one-third each of protein, vegetables, and grains—all of these meals contain these three food groups in calorie-controlled portions. Your options for lunch and dinner vary from prepared dishes, to vegetarian courses, to frozen meals. "A," "B," and "C" snacks follow the dinner section.

Choose one item from each of the following lists.

Breakfast

Each breakfast contains about 250 calories. You get a minimum of 5 grams of fiber, as well as at least 250 milligrams (mg) of calcium—equivalent to 25 percent of your daily needs. An antioxidant-rich fruit is provided with every breakfast option.

- Kashi Heart to Heart cereal (¾ c) topped with sliced strawberries (1 c) and fat-free milk (1 c)
- Whole wheat toast (1 slice) with creamy peanut butter (2 tsp), La Yogurt Light Nonfat yogurt (6 oz), and 1 plum
- Whole Grain Total cereal (¾ c) with blueberries (¾ c) and fat-free milk (1 c)
- Quaker Oatmeal Nutrition for Women (1 packet) made with fat-free milk (⅔ c) and topped with raspberries (½ c) and chopped pecans (1 tsp)
- Thomas' Light Multigrain English muffin (1) with part-skim ricotta (¼ cup) and ground cinnamon sprinkled on top (1 tsp) and fresh blueberries (¾ c)
- Kashi Go Lean cereal (¾ c) with Colombo Fat Free Light yogurt (8 oz) and cranberries (1 c)

- Low-fat bran muffin (½) with Dannon Light 'n Fit yogurt (6 oz) topped with slivered almonds (1 T) and blueberries (1 T)
- Spinach omelet (3 egg whites, ½ cup cooked spinach, and ½ oz low-fat cheddar cheese), whole wheat toast (1 slice), and blackberries (1 c)
- Kashi Go Lean waffle (1) spread with low-fat cottage cheese with calcium (Light n' Lively) (¾ c) and strawberries (1 c)
- Whole wheat bagel (such as Thomas') (½) with Laughing Cow Light Swiss cheese spread (1 wedge), small Red Delicious or Gala apple (4 oz), and fat-free milk (4 oz)
- Kellogg's Complete Bran Flakes (¾ c) with wheat germ (3 tsp) topped with raspberries (¾ c) and fat-free milk (1 c)
- Quaker Oatmeal Squares cereal (¾ c) with sliced strawberries (½ c) and fat-free milk (1 c)
- Pria Complete Nutrition Bar and medium Red Delicious or Gala apple (5 oz)
- Whole wheat bagel (such as Thomas') (½) with Philadelphia Fat Free Garden Vegetable Soft Cream Cheese (2 T) and lox (2 oz), and mixed berries (¼ c blackberries and ¼ c raspberries)

Lunch

Your lunches provide about 350 calories. They also contain a minimum of 6 grams of fiber. Note that each meal is approximately one-third protein, one-third grains, and one-third vegetables.

- Tuna (3 oz) on a whole wheat pita with mixed greens, shredded carrot, tomato, and cucumber (1 c) with Annie's Naturals Balsamic Vinaigrette dressing (1 T)
- Chicken salad (2 oz) made with Dijon mustard (1 T) on whole wheat bread (2 slices), and mixed greens, shredded carrot, tomato, and cucumber (1 c) with Annie's Naturals Low-Fat Raspberry Vinaigrette dressing (2 T)

- Shrimp salad: Large shrimp (10, 2 oz) with blue (or other crumbled) cheese (1 oz) on mixed greens, shredded carrot, tomato, and cucumber (1 c) with Newman's Own Light Raspberry & Walnut Vinaigrette (2 T), and small whole wheat roll (1½ oz)
- Open-face veggie burger: Garden vegetable burger (Morningstar Farms) with low-fat Muenster cheese (1-oz slice) and slice of tomato on whole wheat bread (1 slice), and Health Valley 14 Garden Vegetable soup, fat-free (1 c)
- Thomas' Whole Wheat Sahara Wrap (½) filled with oven-roasted turkey breast (3 oz), reduced-fat Swiss cheese (Sargento thin slice) (1 oz), romaine lettuce (2 leaves), slice of tomato, and honey mustard (1 T), and mixed greens, shredded carrot, tomato, and cucumber (1 c) with Annie's Naturals Balsamic Vinaigrette dressing (1 T)
- Tuna maki (6 pieces), yellowtail sashimi (1 oz), and salmon sashimi (1 oz) with wasabi (1 tsp) and pickled ginger (2 T), and mixed greens, shredded carrot, tomato, and cucumber (1 c) with Annie's Naturals Low-Fat Gingerly Vinaigrette dressing (1 T)
- Whole wheat pita filled with hummus (¼ c), reduced-fat Swiss cheese (Sargento thin slice) (1 oz), chopped arugula (½ c), tomato (2 slices), chopped carrots (¼ c), and sprouts (½ c)
- Poached salmon (3 oz) with light mayonnaise (2 tsp) and dill (1 tsp) over spinach salad (1 c) with red onion (⅛ c), cherry tomatoes (5), red bell pepper (¼ c), and mandarin oranges (¼ c) with Kraft Fat-Free Red Wine Vinegar dressing (2 T), and Wasa Rye Crispbread (2)
- Health Valley 3 Bean Mild Vegetarian Chili (1½ c) topped with shredded reduced-fat cheddar cheese (1½ T), with mixed greens, shredded carrot, tomato, and cucumber (1 c) with Newman's Own Light Balsamic Vinaigrette dressing (1 T), and Wasa Rye Crispbread (1)
- Chicken Greek salad: Grilled chicken breast (2 oz), feta cheese (1½ oz), and black olives (4) over mixed salad greens

(1 c) with red onion (⅛ c), cherry tomatoes (5), red bell pepper (¼ c), and cucumber (¼ c) with Kraft Fat-Free Red Wine Vinegar dressing (2 T), and small whole wheat pita (or ½ large)

- Tuna (2 oz) on Thomas' Light Multigrain English muffin (1) topped with melted reduced-fat Swiss cheese (Sargento thin slice) (1 oz) and sliced tomato (2), and mixed greens, shredded carrot, tomato, and cucumber (1 c), and raisins (1 T) with Annie's Naturals Low-Fat Raspberry Vinaigrette (2 T)
- Oven-roasted turkey breast (2 oz) on whole wheat bread (2 slices) with low-fat Muenster cheese (1 oz), spinach leaves (2), tomato (2 slices), and honey mustard (1 T)
- Campbell's Chunky Chicken Noodle soup (1 c), with mixed greens, shredded carrot, tomato, and cucumber (1 c) topped with Gruyère cheese (1 oz) with Annie's Naturals Low-Fat Raspberry Vinaigrette dressing (2 T), and Wasa Rye Crispbread (2)
- Lean Cuisine Spa Cuisine Chicken in Peanut Sauce frozen entree and baby spinach salad (1 c) with red onion (⅛ c), cherry tomatoes (5), red bell pepper (¼ c), yellow bell pepper (¼ c), and cucumber (¼ c) with Kraft Fat-Free Red Wine Vinegar dressing (2 T)

Dinner

Your dinners provide about 350 calories. Note that each meal contains about one-third protein, one-third grains, and one-third vegetables.

- Broiled salmon fillet (4 oz) with light mayonnaise (1 tsp) and Dijon mustard (1 T), wild rice (½ c), and steamed zucchini and squash (1 c)
- Grilled chicken breast (3 oz), sautéed broccoli (1 c, using 1 tsp olive oil, 2 T dry white wine, ½ clove garlic, 2 tsp golden raisins, and red pepper flakes), and couscous (½ c)
- Sautéed mixed vegetables (1 c zucchini, ½ c mushrooms, ¼ c water chestnuts, ¼ c green onion, 1 clove garlic, 2 tsp

olive oil, and 2 tsp light teriyaki sauce), grilled shrimp (15), and brown rice (½ c)

- Grilled striped bass (3 oz) covered in mixed dried herbs (2 tsp), sautéed spinach (1 c, using 1 tsp olive oil), and orzo (½ c, 1½ oz dry)
- Honey mustard chicken (4 oz) (marinate chicken in 2 tsp Dijon mustard, 1¼ tsp honey, and 1½ tsp reduced-sodium soy sauce), wild rice (½ c), and sautéed broccoli and carrots (1 c, using 1 tsp olive oil)
- Broiled tilapia fillet (3 oz) seasoned with lemon juice (1 T), Worcestershire sauce (¼ tsp), and paprika (1 tsp), medium baked sweet potato (4 oz), and sautéed broccoli rabe (4 oz, using 2 tsp olive oil)
- Trout (4 oz) baked with onion (¼ c), bell pepper (½ c), mushrooms (½ c), diced black olives (4), and stewed tomatoes (3½ oz) over whole wheat pasta (½ c)
- Turkey fajitas: Turkey breast (3 oz) marinated in lemon juice (1½ tsp), rice vinegar (¾ tsp), Worcestershire sauce (¾ tsp), salt, black pepper, cumin, crushed coriander (¾ tsp), and minced garlic (½ clove) and then sautéed (using vegetable oil cooking spray and 1 tsp olive oil) with red bell pepper (¼ c), onion (¼ c), carrot (¼ c), and tomato (¼ c), served in whole wheat tortilla (6"–8") with salsa (2 T) and guacamole (2 T)
- Chinese takeout: Steamed chicken breast (3 oz) with steamed veggies (1 c mix broccoli, carrots, and water chestnuts), brown sauce (1 T, ½ oz), and steamed brown rice (½ c)
- Roasted halibut (3 oz) over asparagus (8 spears) (tossed with 1 tsp olive oil), topped with red pepper relish (2 T minced red bell pepper, 1 T fresh orange juice, 1 tsp olive oil, and ½ tsp honey), and Near East Wheat Pilaf (½ c, 28 g dry)
- Healthy Choice Meals Sesame Chicken and mixed greens, shredded carrot, tomato, and cucumber (1 c) with balsamic vinegar (1 T)
- Smart Ones Meatloaf with Gravy Entrée and Health Valley Vegetable soup, low-fat (1 c)

- Lean Cuisine Spa Cuisine Salmon with Basil frozen entree and Health Valley Low-Fat Minestrone soup (1 c)
- California Pizza Kitchen Thai Chicken Pizza (2 slices) and spinach salad (1 c) topped with low-fat goat cheese (1 oz), red onion (⅛ c), and beets (¼ c) with red wine vinegar (1 T)

Snacks

The "A," "B," and "C" snacks comprise antiaging snacks (fruits and vegetables rich in antioxidants, including beta-carotene, vitamin C, and vitamin E); bone-building snacks (meeting a quarter of your daily calcium needs); and comfort snacks (sweet or salty "indulgent" snacks, including cookies, sweets, and candy).

ANTIAGING ("A") SNACKS. Each antiaging snack contains about 75 calories. Pick one "A" snack each day.

- Cantaloupe (½ c cubes) with sunflower seeds (1 T)
- Red Delicious apple (4 oz) with creamy peanut butter (1 tsp)
- Raw peanuts (1 T) with dried cranberries (½ oz, about 2 T)
- Blueberries (½ c) with fat-free Cool Whip (1 T) and slivered almonds (1 T)
- Dried apricot halves (4) with walnut halves (4)
- Tangerine (1 medium, about 3 oz) with raw almonds (6)
- Banana (½ medium, about 2 oz) with raw almonds (6)
- Sweet cherries (½ c) with pecans (4 halves)
- Strawberries (½ c) with pecans (5 halves)
- Mixed berries (¼ c blackberries and ¼ c raspberries) with yogurt dressing (2 T) and flaxseeds (2 tsp)
- Plum (1) with dry-roasted edamame (1½ T)
- Prunes (2) with raw almonds (6)
- Crudités of red bell pepper (¼ c) and broccoli florets (5) with hummus (2 T)
- Watermelon (¾ c cubes) with raw peanuts (1 T)

BONE-BUILDING ("B") SNACKS. "B" snacks contain about 100 calories and meet at least a quarter (250 mg) of your daily calcium needs. Each "B" snack also contains at least 5 grams of protein. Pick one each day.

- Starbucks Caffé Misto/Café Au Lait with fat-free milk, grande (16 oz)
- Stonyfield Farm Moove Over Sugar yogurt (4 oz), with All-Bran with Extra Fiber (¼ c)
- Chilled Banana Latte (Mix 1½ T sugar-free crème de banana syrup, 1½ T sugar-free coconut syrup, and 1 c fat-free milk in a 20-oz chilled stainless steel pitcher. Froth milk with whisk until airy and light. Add a shot of espresso and pour over ice.)
- Sargento Light String Cheese Snacks (2)
- Thomas' Light Multigrain English muffin (½) with reduced-fat Swiss cheese (Sargento thin slice) (¾ oz)
- Pria bar (110 calories) or any energy bar with 300 mg calcium, 5 g protein, and up to 125 calories
- Blueberry smoothie (Blend 4 oz fat-free milk, 2 oz fat-free blueberry yogurt, ½ c frozen blueberries, and 1 packet of Splenda on high speed until smooth.)
- Vegetable dip (2 T Lipton-Gefen Vegetable Soup & Dip Mix mixed with ½ c Stonyfield Farm fat-free plain yogurt) and red bell pepper strips (⅓ c)
- Sugar-free hot cocoa mix (1 packet) made with low-fat milk (4 oz) and hot water (4 oz)
- 8th Continent Vanilla Soymilk (8 oz)
- Stonyfield Farm plain low-fat yogurt (6 oz) sprinkled with cinnamon (1 tsp)
- Soyco Cheddar Veggy Singles (1 slice, 30 g) with low-fat whole wheat crackers (Health Valley) (2)
- Cheese kabob: Alternate cubes of low-fat cheddar cheese (2 oz) with yellow bell pepper (¼ c) and cucumber (¼ c)
- Starbucks Iced Caffé Latte with soy milk (tall, 12 oz)

COMFORT ("C") SNACKS. Each comfort snack contains about 75 calories. Pick one "C" snack each day.

- Hershey's Kisses (3)
- Peanut M&Ms (8)
- Nature Valley Peanut Butter Granola Bar (or another flavor) (1)
- Tootsie Roll Midgees (3)
- Nabisco Honey Maid Cinnamon Graham Crackers (1 sheet/ 4 crackers)
- Animal crackers (15)
- Health Valley Low-Fat Amaretto Biscotti Style cookie (1)
- Snyder's Organic Honey Wheat Pretzel Sticks (10)
- 98% fat-free vanilla ice cream (such as Breyers) (½ cup)
- Rice Krispies Treat (1)
- Snackwell's bite-size chocolate chip cookies (8)
- Baked tortilla chips (such as Tostitos) (10) with salsa (¼ c, 2 oz)
- Nabisco 100-calorie pack (Oreo Thin Crisps; Chips Ahoy Thin Crisps; Honey Maid Cinnamon Thin Crisps; Ritz Snack Mix; Planters Peanut Butter Cookie Crisps)
- Fudgsicle No Sugar Added Pops (2, 84 g)

Week 1 Meal Plan

Day 1

BREAKFAST
Kashi Heart to Heart cereal (¾ c) topped with sliced strawberries (1 c) and fat-free milk (1 c)

MIDMORNING "A" SNACK
Raw peanuts (1 T) with dried cranberries (½ oz, about 2 T)

LUNCH
Poached salmon (3 oz) with light mayonnaise (2 tsp) and dill (1 tsp) over spinach salad (1 c) with red onion

(⅛ c), cherry tomatoes (5), red bell pepper (¼ c), and mandarin oranges (¼ c) with Kraft Fat-Free Red Wine Vinegar dressing (2 T), and Wasa Rye Crispbread (2)

AFTERNOON "B" SNACK
Pria bar (110 calories) or any energy bar with 300 mg calcium, 5 g protein, and up to 125 calories

DINNER
Turkey fajitas: Turkey breast (3 oz) marinated in lemon juice (1½ tsp), rice vinegar (¾ tsp), Worcestershire sauce (¾ tsp), salt, black pepper, cumin, crushed coriander (¾ tsp), and minced garlic (½ clove) and then sautéed (using vegetable oil cooking spray and 1 tsp olive oil) with red bell pepper (¼ c), onion (¼ c), carrot (¼ c), and tomato (¼ c), served in whole wheat tortilla (6″–8″) with salsa (2 T) and guacamole (2 T)

EVENING "C" SNACK
Hershey's Kisses (3)

Day 2

BREAKFAST
Whole wheat toast (1 slice) with creamy peanut butter (2 tsp), La Yogurt Light Nonfat yogurt (6 oz), and 1 plum

MIDMORNING "B" SNACK
Soyco Cheddar Veggy Singles (1 slice, 30 g) with low-fat whole wheat crackers (Health Valley) (2)

LUNCH
Chicken salad (2 oz) made with Dijon mustard (1 T) on whole wheat bread (2 slices), and mixed greens, shredded carrot, tomato, and cucumber (1 c) with Annie's Naturals Low-Fat Raspberry Vinaigrette dressing (2 T)

AFTERNOON "A" SNACK

Cantaloupe (½ c cubes) with sunflower seeds (1 T)

DINNER

Broiled tilapia fillet (3 oz) seasoned with lemon juice
(1 T), Worcestershire sauce (¼ tsp), and paprika (1 tsp),
medium baked sweet potato (4 oz), and sautéed broccoli
rabe (4 oz, using 2 tsp olive oil)

EVENING "C" SNACK

Tootsie Roll Midgees (3)

Day 3

BREAKFAST

Whole Grain Total cereal (¾ c) with blueberries (¾ c) and
fat-free milk (1 c)

MIDMORNING "A" SNACK

Dried apricot halves (4) with walnut halves (4)

LUNCH

Chicken Greek salad: Grilled chicken breast (2 oz), feta
cheese (1½ oz), and black olives (4) over mixed salad
greens (1 c) with red onion (⅛ c), cherry tomatoes (5),
red bell pepper (¼ c), and cucumber (¼ c) with Kraft
Fat-Free Red Wine Vinegar dressing (2 T), and small
whole wheat pita (or ½ large)

AFTERNOON "B" SNACK

Starbucks Caffé Misto/Café Au Lait with fat-free milk,
grande (16 oz)

DINNER

Roasted halibut (3 oz) over asparagus (8 spears) (tossed
with 1 tsp olive oil), topped with red pepper relish (2 T
minced red bell pepper, 1 T fresh orange juice, 1 tsp
olive oil, and ½ tsp honey), and Near East Wheat Pilaf
(½ c, 28 g dry)

EVENING "C" SNACK
Nabisco Honey Maid Cinnamon Graham Crackers
(1 sheet/4 crackers)

Day 4

BREAKFAST
Quaker Oatmeal Nutrition for Women (1 packet) made with
fat-free milk (⅔ c) and topped with raspberries (½ c) and
chopped pecans (1 tsp)

MIDMORNING "B" SNACK
8th Continent Vanilla Soymilk (8 oz)

LUNCH
Lean Cuisine Spa Cuisine Chicken in Peanut Sauce frozen
entree and baby spinach salad (1 c) with red onion (⅛ c),
cherry tomatoes (5), red bell pepper (¼ c), yellow bell
pepper (¼ c), and cucumber (¼ c) with Kraft Fat-Free
Red Wine Vinegar dressing (2 T)

AFTERNOON "A" SNACK
Banana (½ medium, about 2 oz) with raw almonds (6)

DINNER
Broiled salmon fillet (4 oz) with light mayonnaise (1 tsp)
and Dijon mustard (1 T), wild rice (½ c), and steamed
zucchini and squash (1 c)

EVENING "C" SNACK
Baked tortilla chips (such as Tostitos) (10) with salsa (¼ c,
2 oz)

Day 5

BREAKFAST
Thomas' Light Multigrain English muffin (1) with part-skim
ricotta (¼ cup) and ground cinnamon sprinkled on top
(1 tsp) and fresh blueberries (¾ c)

MIDMORNING "A" SNACK
Strawberries (½ c) with pecans (5 halves)

LUNCH
Health Valley 3 Bean Mild Vegetarian Chili (1½ c) topped
   with shredded reduced-fat cheddar cheese (1½ T), with
   mixed greens, shredded carrot, tomato, and cucumber
   (1 c) with Newman's Own Light Balsamic Vinaigrette
   dressing (1 T), and Wasa Rye Crispbread (1)

AFTERNOON "B" SNACK
Sargento Light String Cheese Snacks (2)

DINNER
Healthy Choice Meals Sesame Chicken and mixed greens,
   shredded carrot, tomato, and cucumber (1 c) with
   balsamic vinegar (1 T)

EVENING "C" SNACK
Snackwell's bite-size chocolate chip cookies (8)

Day 6

BREAKFAST
Kashi Go Lean cereal (¾ c) with Colombo Fat Free Light
   yogurt (8 oz) and cranberries (1 c)

MIDMORNING "B" SNACK
Chilled Banana Latte (Mix 1½ T sugar-free crème de
   banana syrup, 1½ T sugar-free coconut syrup, and 1 c
   fat-free milk in a 20-oz chilled stainless steel pitcher.
   Froth milk with whisk until airy and light. Add a shot of
   espresso and pour over ice.)

LUNCH
Shrimp salad: Large shrimp (10, 2 oz) with blue (or other
   crumbled) cheese (1 oz) on mixed greens, shredded
   carrot, tomato, and cucumber (1 c) with Newman's Own

Light Raspberry & Walnut Vinaigrette (2 T), and small whole wheat roll (1½ oz)

AFTERNOON "A" SNACK

Tangerine (1 medium, about 3 oz) with raw almonds (6)

DINNER

Chinese takeout: Steamed chicken breast (3 oz) with steamed veggies (1 c mix broccoli, carrots, and water chestnuts), brown sauce (1 T, ½ oz), and steamed brown rice (½ c)

EVENING "C" SNACK

Health Valley Low-Fat Amaretto Biscotti Style cookie (1)

Day 7

BREAKFAST

Whole wheat bagel (such as Thomas') (½) with Laughing Cow Light Swiss cheese spread (1 wedge), small Red Delicious or Gala apple (4 oz), and fat-free milk (4 oz)

MIDMORNING "B" SNACK

Stonyfield Farm plain low-fat yogurt (6 oz) sprinkled with cinnamon (1 tsp)

LUNCH

Tuna (2 oz) on Thomas' Light Multigrain English muffin (1) topped with melted reduced-fat Swiss cheese (Sargento thin slice) (1 oz) and sliced tomato (2), and mixed greens, shredded carrot, tomato, and cucumber (1 c), and raisins (1 T) with Annie's Naturals Low-Fat Raspberry Vinaigrette (2 T)

AFTERNOON "A" SNACK

Crudités of red bell pepper (¼ c) and broccoli florets (5) with hummus (2 T)

DINNER

California Pizza Kitchen Thai Chicken Pizza (2 slices) and
  spinach salad (1 c) topped with low-fat goat cheese (1 oz),
  red onion (⅛ c), and beets (¼ c) with red wine vinegar
  (1 T)

EVENING "C" SNACK

Animal crackers (15)

AVERAGES FOR THE WEEK*

1,225 calories
51% carbohydrate (28 grams of fiber)
25% protein
24% fat (6% saturated)
1,205 milligrams of calcium

Week 2 Meal Plan

Day 8

BREAKFAST

Low-fat bran muffin (½) with Dannon Light 'n Fit
  yogurt (6 oz) topped with slivered almonds (1 T) and
  blueberries (1 T)

MIDMORNING "A" SNACK

Watermelon (¾ c cubes) with raw peanuts (1 T)

LUNCH

Campbell's Chunky Chicken Noodle soup (1 c), mixed
  greens, shredded carrot, tomato, and cucumber (1 c)
  topped with Gruyère cheese (1 oz) with Annie's Naturals
  Low-Fat Raspberry Vinaigrette dressing (2 T), and Wasa
  Rye Crispbread (2)

---

*Calculated using The Food Processor software, ESHA Research,
Salem, Oregon

AFTERNOON "B" SNACK

Cheese kabob: Alternate cubes of low-fat cheddar cheese
  (2 oz) with yellow bell pepper (¼ c) and cucumber (¼ c)

DINNER

Trout (4 oz) baked with onion (¼ c), bell pepper (½ c),
  mushrooms (½ c), diced black olives (4), and stewed
  tomatoes (3½ oz) over whole wheat pasta (½ c)

EVENING "C" SNACK

Snyder's Organic Honey Wheat Pretzel Sticks (10)

Day 9

BREAKFAST

Spinach omelet (3 egg whites, ½ cup cooked spinach, and
  ½ oz low-fat cheddar cheese), whole wheat toast (1 slice),
  and blackberries (1 c)

MIDMORNING "A" SNACK

Sweet cherries (½ c) with pecans (4 halves)

LUNCH

Tuna (3 oz) on a whole wheat pita with mixed greens,
  shredded carrot, tomato, and cucumber (1 c) with
  Annie's Naturals Balsamic Vinaigrette dressing (1 T)

AFTERNOON "B" SNACK

Stonyfield Farm Moove Over Sugar yogurt (4 oz), with All-
  Bran with Extra Fiber (¼ c)

DINNER

Lean Cuisine Spa Cuisine Salmon with Basil frozen entree
  and Health Valley Low-Fat Minestrone soup (1 c)

EVENING "C" SNACK

Peanut M&Ms (8)

Day 10

BREAKFAST

Kashi Go Lean waffle (1) spread with low-fat cottage cheese with calcium (Light n' Lively) (¾ c) and strawberries (1 c)

MIDMORNING "B" SNACK

Starbucks Iced Caffé Latte with soy milk (tall, 12 oz)

LUNCH

Oven-roasted turkey breast (2 oz) on whole wheat bread (2 slices) with low-fat Muenster cheese (1 oz), spinach leaves (2), tomato (2 slices), and honey mustard (1 T)

AFTERNOON "A" SNACK

Prunes (2) with raw almonds (6)

DINNER

Honey mustard chicken (4 oz) (marinate chicken in 2 tsp Dijon mustard, 1¼ tsp honey, and 1½ tsp reduced-sodium soy sauce), wild rice (½ c), and sautéed broccoli and carrots (1 c, using 1 tsp olive oil)

EVENING "C" SNACK

Nature Valley Peanut Butter Granola Bar (or another flavor) (1)

Day 11

BREAKFAST

Kellogg's Complete Bran Flakes (¾ c) with wheat germ (3 tsp) topped with raspberries (¾ c) and fat-free milk (1 c)

MIDMORNING "B" SNACK

Sugar-free hot cocoa mix (1 packet) made with low-fat milk (4 oz) and hot water (4 oz)

LUNCH

Thomas' Whole Wheat Sahara Wrap (½) filled with oven-roasted turkey breast (3 oz), reduced-fat Swiss cheese (Sargento thin slice) (1 oz), romaine lettuce (2 leaves), slice of tomato, and honey mustard (1 T), and mixed greens, shredded carrot, tomato, and cucumber (1 c) with Annie's Naturals Balsamic Vinaigrette dressing (1 T)

AFTERNOON "A" SNACK

Plums (1) with dry-roasted edamame (1½ T)

DINNER

Sautéed mixed vegetables (1 c zucchini, ½ c mushrooms, ¼ c water chestnuts, ¼ c green onion, 1 clove garlic, 2 tsp olive oil, and 2 tsp light teriyaki sauce), grilled shrimp (15), and brown rice (½ c)

EVENING "C" SNACK

Rice Krispies Treat (1)

Day 12

BREAKFAST

Quaker Oatmeal Squares cereal (¾ c) with sliced strawberries (½ c) and fat-free milk (1 c)

MIDMORNING "A" SNACK

Mixed berries (¼ c blackberries and ¼ c raspberries) with yogurt dressing (2 T) and flaxseeds (2 tsp)

LUNCH

Whole wheat pita filled with hummus (¼ c), reduced-fat Swiss cheese (Sargento thin slice) (1 oz), chopped arugula (½ c), tomato (2 slices), chopped carrot (¼ c), and sprouts (½ c)

AFTERNOON "B" SNACK

Thomas' Light Multigrain English muffin (½) with reduced-fat Swiss cheese (Sargento thin slice) (¾ oz)

DINNER

Grilled striped bass (3 oz) covered in mixed dried herbs (2 tsp), sautéed spinach (1 c, using 1 tsp olive oil), and orzo (½ c, 1½ oz dry)

EVENING "C" SNACK

Nabisco 100-calorie pack (Oreo Thin Crisps; Chips Ahoy Thin Crisps; Honey Maid Cinnamon Thin Crisps; Ritz Snack Mix; Planters Peanut Butter Cookie Crisps)

Day 13

BREAKFAST

Pria Complete Nutrition Bar with medium Red Delicious or Gala apple (5 oz)

MIDMORNING "A" SNACK

Blueberries (½ c) with fat-free Cool Whip (1 T) and slivered almonds (1 T)

LUNCH

Open-face veggie burger: Garden vegetable burger (Morningstar Farms) with low-fat Muenster cheese (1-oz slice) and slice of tomato on whole wheat bread (1 slice), and Health Valley 14 Garden Vegetable, fat-free soup (1 c)

AFTERNOON "B" SNACK

Vegetable dip (2 T Lipton-Gefen Vegetable Soup & Dip Mix mixed with ½ c Stonyfield Farm fat-free plain yogurt) and red bell pepper strips (⅓ c)

DINNER

Grilled chicken breast (3 oz), sautéed broccoli (1 c, using 1 tsp olive oil, 2 T dry white wine, ½ clove garlic, 2 tsp golden raisins, and red pepper flakes), and couscous (½ c)

EVENING "C" SNACK
Fudgsicle No Sugar Added Pops (2, 84 g)

Day 14

BREAKFAST
Whole wheat bagel (such as Thomas') (½) with Philadelphia Fat Free Garden Vegetable Soft Cream Cheese (2 T) and lox (2 oz), and mixed berries (¼ c blackberries and ¼ c raspberries)

MIDMORNING "B" SNACK
Blueberry smoothie (Blend 4 oz fat-free milk, 2 oz fat-free blueberry yogurt, ½ c frozen blueberries, and 1 packet of Splenda on high speed until smooth.)

LUNCH
Tuna maki (6 pieces), yellowtail sashimi (1 oz), and salmon sashimi (1 oz) with wasabi (1 tsp) and pickled ginger (2 T), and mixed greens, shredded carrot, tomato, and cucumber (1 c) with Annie's Naturals Low-Fat Gingerly Vinaigrette dressing (1 T)

AFTERNOON "A" SNACK
Red Delicious apple (4 oz) with creamy peanut butter (1 tsp)

DINNER
Smart Ones Meatloaf with Gravy Entrée and Health Valley Vegetable soup, low-fat (1 c)

EVENING "C" SNACK
98% fat-free vanilla ice cream (½ cup) (such as Breyers)

AVERAGES FOR THE WEEK*
1,254 calories
52% carbohydrate (31 grams of fiber)
26% protein
22% fat (6% saturated)
1,117 milligrams of calcium

Shopping List for 1,200-Calorie Meal Plan

FRUITS
Strawberries
Blueberries
Raspberries
Blackberries
Fresh whole cranberries
Red Delicious or Gala apples (small and medium)
Plums
Cantaloupe
Tangerines
Bananas
Sweet cherries
Watermelon
Dried cranberries
Dried apricot halves
Raisins (black and golden)
Prunes
Juice oranges or fresh-squeezed orange juice

---

*Calculated using The Food Processor software, ESHA Research, Salem, Oregon

VEGETABLES
Asparagus
Baby spinach
Mixed salad greens
Red onion
Cherry tomatoes
Tomatoes
Yellow bell peppers
Red bell peppers
Carrots (whole, shredded, and baby)
Cucumber
Spinach
Romaine lettuce leaves
Arugula
Sprouts
Squash
Zucchini
Broccoli
Mushrooms
Water chestnuts
Green onions
Sweet potatoes (medium)
Broccoli rabe
Garlic

BREADS, GRAINS, AND CEREALS
Kashi Heart to Heart cereal
Kashi Go Lean cereal
Whole Grain Total cereal
Kellogg's Complete Bran Flakes
Quaker Oatmeal Squares cereal
All-Bran with Extra Fiber cereal
Quaker Oatmeal Nutrition for Women
Thomas' Light Multigrain English muffin
Low-fat bran muffin
Kashi Go Lean waffle

Thomas' whole wheat bagel

Wheat germ

Whole wheat pita (small and large)

Small whole wheat rolls (about 1½ oz each)

Thomas' Whole Wheat Sahara Wraps (or similar whole wheat wrap)

Wasa Rye Crispbread

Whole wheat tortilla

Stroehmann 100% whole wheat bread (3 g fiber, 70–90 calories per slice)

Health Valley low-fat whole wheat crackers

Wild rice

Couscous

Brown rice

Orzo

Whole wheat pasta

Near East Wheat Pilaf

Flaxseeds

DAIRY PRODUCTS (MILK, CHEESE, EGGS)

Fat-free milk

Low-fat (1%) milk

8th Continent Vanilla Soymilk

La Yogurt Light Nonfat, Dannon Light 'n Fit, or Colombo Fat Free Light yogurt

Stonyfield Farm Moove Over Sugar yogurt

Fat-free blueberry yogurt

Stonyfield Farm fat-free plain yogurt

Stonyfield Farm or Dannon low-fat plain yogurt

Part-skim ricotta cheese

Eggs (use only egg whites)

Low-fat cheddar cheese (shredded and whole)

Light n' Lively low-fat cottage cheese with calcium

Laughing Cow Light Swiss cheese spread (wedges)

Philadelphia Fat-Free Garden Vegetable Soft Cream Cheese

Blue cheese (or other crumbled cheese)

Low-fat Muenster cheese
Sargento thin slice reduced-fat Swiss cheese
Feta cheese
Gruyère cheese
Low-fat goat cheese
Soyco Cheddar Veggy Singles cheese slices
Sargento Light String Cheese Snacks

MEAT, FISH, POULTRY
Lox
Canned tuna fish in water
Chicken breasts (skinless)
Large shrimp
Oven-roasted turkey breast
Salmon fillets (wild, Alaskan)
Striped bass fillet
Tilapia fillet
Trout fillet
Halibut fillet (Alaskan or Pacific)

SUSHI
Tuna maki
Yellowtail sashimi
Salmon sashimi

FROZEN FOODS
Frozen blueberries
Morningstar Farms garden vegetable burgers
Lean Cuisine Spa Cuisine Chicken in Peanut Sauce
Lean Cuisine Spa Cuisine Salmon with Basil
Healthy Choice Meals Sesame Chicken
Smart Ones Meatloaf with Gravy Entrée
California Pizza Kitchen Thai Chicken Pizza
Fat-free Cool Whip

CANNED AND PACKAGED GOODS
Health Valley 14 Garden Vegetable soup, fat-free
Health Valley 3 Bean Mild Vegetarian Chili

Health Valley Vegetable soup, low-fat
Health Valley Low-Fat Minestrone soup
Campbell's Chunky Chicken Noodle soup
Lipton-Gefen Vegetable Soup & Dip Mix
Mandarin oranges
Stewed tomatoes (3½-oz can)
Salsa
Canned beets
Sugar-free hot cocoa packets

SNACKS

Hershey's Kisses
Peanut M&Ms
Nature Valley Granola Bars
Rice Krispies Treats
Tootsie Roll Midgees
Nabisco Honey Maid Cinnamon Graham Crackers
Animal crackers
Nabisco 100-calorie packs
Snackwell's bite-size chocolate chip cookies
Health Valley Low-Fat Amaretto Biscotti Style cookies
Snyder's Organic Honey Wheat Pretzel Sticks
Tostitos baked tortilla chips
Breyers 98% fat-free vanilla ice cream
Fudgsicle No Sugar Added Pops

FATS AND OILS

Olive oil
Pam cooking spray
Creamy peanut butter
Raw peanuts
Sunflower seeds
Chopped pecans
Pecan halves
Slivered almonds
Raw almonds

Walnut halves
Black olives

SALAD DRESSINGS
Kraft Fat-Free Red Wine Vinegar
Annie's Naturals Low-Fat Raspberry Vinaigrette
Annie's Naturals Balsamic Vinaigrette
Annie's Naturals Low-Fat Gingerly Vinaigrette
Newman's Own Light Raspberry & Walnut Vinaigrette
Newman's Own Light Balsamic Vinaigrette

CONDIMENTS
Light mayonnaise
Lemon juice
Rice vinegar
Worcestershire sauce
Brown sauce
Guacamole
Dijon mustard
Honey mustard
Light teriyaki sauce
Honey
Low-sodium soy sauce
Balsamic vinegar
Red wine vinegar
Wasabi
Pickled ginger

HERBS AND SPICES
Salt
Black pepper
Dill
Cumin
Crushed coriander
Paprika
Ground cinnamon

Red pepper flakes
Dried herbs (e.g., basil, oregano)

MISCELLANEOUS

Pria 110 Plus energy bar (up to 125 calories, 300 mg calcium,
   5 g protein)
Pria Complete Nutrition energy bar (up to 170 calories,
   400 mg calcium, 11 g protein)
Espresso
Dry-roasted edamame
Hummus
Splenda (packet)
Dry white wine (for cooking)
Sugar-free crème de banana syrup
Sugar-free coconut syrup

The 1,400-
Calorie Meal Plan

(7)

The 1,400-calorie plan is appropriate if you're just getting into an exercise routine and your goal is to exercise once or twice a week, for about 20 to 30 minutes each session. The 1,400-calorie plan is also a good starting point if you are currently exercising this much. If you find that you are hungry and need more calories, you can always transition to the 1,600-calorie plan. If, after a few weeks, you're not losing any weight, I recommend increasing the amount or intensity of your exercise. If you are not currently exercising and are having difficulty losing weight on the 1,400-calorie plan, you can switch to the 1,200-calorie plan.

I've given you two basic ways to follow your plan: You can choose individual breakfast, lunch, dinner, and snack fare from the lists in the first part of this chapter, or you can follow the chapter's complete two-week meal plan. The options format works well if you want to have total flexibility with your meal and snack choices each day, whereas the meal plan format gives you more structure.

Please note that while brand names are often cited, they are *only* suggestions for what can be included on your plan. You can feel free to substitute other foods wherever you like, as long as the number of calories is the same. Also, see Appendix A for substitution lists.

Options Format

Your breakfasts comprise one serving of fruit (mostly the "antiaging" fruits, which are loaded with antioxidants) and one bone-building ("B") food. Each breakfast also contains a source of whole grains or other fiber-rich food and has a moderate amount of protein. Lunch and dinner plates can be visualized as one-third each of protein, vegetables, and grains—these meals contain the three food groups in calorie-controlled portions. Your options for lunch and dinner vary from prepared dishes, to vegetarian courses, to frozen meals. Options for "A," "B," and "C" snacks are presented after the dinner listings.

Choose one selection from each of these six lists each day.

Breakfast

Each breakfast contains about 300 calories. It provides a minimum of 5 grams of fiber and at least 250 milligrams (mg) of calcium, giving you 25 percent of your daily needs. An antioxidant-rich fruit is also part of every breakfast option.

- Kashi Heart to Heart cereal (1 c) topped with sliced strawberries (1 c), wheat germ (2 tsp), and fat-free milk (1 c)
- Whole wheat toast (1 slice) with creamy peanut butter (1 T), La Yogurt Light Nonfat yogurt (6 oz), and 1 plum
- Whole Grain Total cereal (1 c) with blueberries (¾ c) and fat-free milk (1 c)
- Whole wheat bagel (such as Thomas') (½) with Laughing Cow Light Swiss cheese spread (2 wedges), medium Red Delicious or Gala apple, and fat-free milk (4 oz)
- Quaker Oatmeal Nutrition for Women (1 packet) made with fat-free milk (⅔ c) and topped with raspberries (½ c) and chopped pecans (1 T)

- Thomas' Light Multigrain English muffin (1) with part-skim ricotta (¼ c) and ground cinnamon sprinkled on top (1 tsp) and fresh blueberries (1 c)
- Kashi Go Lean cereal (1 c) with Colombo Fat Free Light yogurt (8 oz) and cranberries (1 c)
- Low-fat bran muffin (½) with Dannon Light 'n Fit yogurt (6 oz) and blackberries (1 c)
- Spinach omelet (4 egg whites, ½ cup cooked spinach, and ½ oz low-fat cheddar cheese), whole wheat toast (1 slice), and medium Red Delicious or Gala apple
- Kashi Go Lean waffle (1) spread with low-fat cottage cheese with calcium (Light n' Lively) (½ c) and low-sugar jelly (1 T), and strawberries (1 c) with fat-free milk (4 oz)
- Kellogg's Complete Bran Flakes (¾ c) and Fiber One (½ c) topped with raspberries (¾ c) and fat-free milk (1 c)
- Quaker Oatmeal Squares cereal (¾ c) with sliced strawberries (1 c) and fat-free milk (1 c)
- Silk Live! Soy raspberry smoothie with raw almonds (6) and 1 plum
- Whole wheat bagel (such as Thomas') (½) with Philadelphia Fat Free Garden Vegetable Soft Cream Cheese (2 T) and lox (2 oz), and mixed berries (½ c blackberries and ½ c raspberries)

Lunch

Your lunches provide about 400 calories. They also contain a minimum of 6 grams of fiber. Note that each meal is approximately one-third protein, one-third grains, and one-third vegetables.

- Tuna (3 oz) with light mayonnaise (2 tsp) on a whole wheat pita with mixed greens, shredded carrot, tomato, and cucumber (1 c) with Annie's Naturals Balsamic Vinaigrette dressing (1 T)
- Chicken salad (3 oz) made with Dijon mustard (2 T) on whole wheat bread (2 slices), and mixed greens, shredded carrot,

tomato, and cucumber (1 c) with low-fat dressing (balsamic vinegar) (2 T)

- Shrimp salad: Large shrimp (10, 2 oz) with blue (or other crumbled) cheese (1 oz) on mixed greens, shredded carrot, tomato, and cucumber (1 c) with peas (¼ c) and Newman's Own Light Raspberry & Walnut Vinaigrette (2 T), and small whole wheat roll (1½ oz)

- Garden vegetable burger (Morningstar Farms) with low-fat Muenster cheese (1-oz slice) and slice of tomato on whole wheat bun (1½ oz), and Health Valley 14 Garden Vegetable soup, fat-free (1 c)

- Thomas' Whole Wheat Sahara Wrap (½) filled with oven-roasted turkey breast (3 oz), reduced-fat Swiss cheese (Sargento thin slice) (1 slice), romaine lettuce (2 leaves), avocado (2 T), slice of tomato, and honey mustard (1 T), and mixed greens, shredded carrot, tomato, and cucumber (1 c) with Annie's Naturals Balsamic Vinaigrette dressing (1 T)

- Tuna maki (6 pieces), yellowtail sashimi (1 oz), salmon sashimi (1 oz), and edamame (½ c not in pod) with wasabi (1 tsp) and pickled ginger (2 T), and mixed greens, shredded carrot, tomato, and cucumber (1 c) with Annie's Naturals Low-Fat Gingerly Vinaigrette dressing (1 T)

- Whole wheat pita filled with hummus (⅓ c), reduced-fat Swiss cheese (Sargento thin slice) (1 oz), avocado (1 T), chopped arugula (½ c), tomato (2 slices), chopped carrot (¼ c), and sprouts (½ c)

- Poached salmon (3 oz) with light mayonnaise (2 tsp) and dill (1 tsp) over spinach salad (1 c) with red onion (⅛ c), cherry tomatoes (5), red bell pepper (¼ c), and mandarin oranges (¼ c) with Kraft Fat-Free Red Wine Vinegar dressing (2 T), and small whole wheat roll (1½ oz)

- Health Valley 3 Bean Mild Vegetarian Chili (1½ c) topped with shredded reduced-fat cheddar cheese (2 T) and nonfat sour cream (1 T), with mixed greens, shredded carrot, tomato, and cucumber (1 c) with Newman's Own Light Balsamic Vinaigrette dressing (2 T), and Wasa Rye Crispbread (1)

- Chicken Greek salad: Grilled chicken breast (2 oz), feta cheese (1½ oz), and black olives (8) over mixed salad greens (1 c) with red onion (⅛ c), cherry tomatoes (5), red bell pepper (¼ c), and cucumber (¼ c) with Kraft Fat-Free Red Wine Vinegar dressing (2 T), and small whole wheat pita (or ½ large)
- Tuna (2 oz) on Thomas' Light Multigrain English muffin (1) topped with melted reduced-fat Swiss cheese (Sargento thin slice) (1 oz) and sliced tomato (2), and mixed greens, shredded carrot, tomato, and cucumber (1 c), raisins (1 T), and sunflower seeds (1 T) with fat-free raspberry vinaigrette (2 T)
- Oven-roasted turkey breast (3 oz) on whole wheat bread (2 slices) with low-fat Muenster cheese (1 oz), spinach leaves (2), tomato (2 slices), and honey mustard (1 T)
- Campbell's Chunky Chicken Vegetable soup (1½ c, 12 oz); mixed greens, shredded carrot, tomato, and cucumber (1 c) topped with Gruyère cheese (½ oz) and grilled chicken breast (1 oz) with Kraft Fat-Free Red Wine Vinegar dressing (2 T); and small whole wheat roll (1½ oz)
- Lean Cuisine Spa Cuisine Chicken in Peanut Sauce frozen entree and baby spinach salad (1 c) with red onion (⅛ c), cherry tomatoes (5), red bell pepper (¼ c), yellow bell pepper (¼ c), cucumber (¼ c), and raw peanuts (1 T) with Kraft Fat-Free Red Wine Vinegar dressing (2 T)

Dinner

Your dinners provide about 400 calories. Note that each meal contains approximately one-third protein, one-third grains, and one-third vegetables.

- Broiled salmon fillet (4 oz) with light mayonnaise (1 tsp) and Dijon mustard (1 T), wild rice (½ c), and steamed zucchini and squash (1 c)
- Grilled chicken breast (4 oz), sautéed broccoli (1 c, using 1 tsp olive oil, 2 T dry white wine, ½ clove garlic, 2 tsp golden raisins, and red pepper flakes), and couscous (½ c)

- Sautéed mixed vegetables (1 c zucchini, ½ c mushrooms, ¼ c water chestnuts, ¼ c green onion, ¼ c corn, 1 clove garlic, 2 tsp olive oil, and 2 tsp light teriyaki sauce), grilled shrimp (15), and brown rice (½ c)
- Grilled striped bass (4 oz) covered in mixed dried herbs (2 tsp), sautéed spinach (1 c, using 1 tsp olive oil), and orzo (½ c, 1½ oz dry) with peas (¼ c)
- Honey mustard chicken (4 oz) (marinate chicken in 2 tsp Dijon mustard, 1¼ tsp honey, and 1½ tsp reduced-sodium soy sauce), wild rice (½ c), and steamed broccoli and carrots (1½ c)
- Broiled tilapia fillet (4 oz) seasoned with lemon juice (1 T), Worcestershire sauce (¼ tsp), and paprika (1 tsp), medium baked sweet potato (4 oz), and sautéed broccoli rabe (4 oz, using 2 tsp olive oil)
- Trout (4 oz) baked with onion (¼ c), bell pepper (½ c), mushrooms (½ c), diced black olives (4), and stewed tomatoes (3½ oz) over whole wheat pasta (½ c)
- Turkey fajitas: Turkey breast (4 oz) marinated in lemon juice (1½ tsp), rice vinegar (¾ tsp), Worcestershire sauce (¾ tsp), salt, black pepper, cumin, crushed coriander (¾ tsp), and minced garlic (½ clove) and then sautéed (using vegetable oil cooking spray and 1 tsp olive oil) with red bell pepper (¼ c), onion (¼ c), carrot (¼ c), and tomato (¼ c), served in whole wheat tortilla (6″–8″) with salsa (2 T) and guacamole (2 T)
- Chinese takeout: Steamed chicken breast (3 oz) with steamed veggies (1 c mix broccoli, carrots, and water chestnuts and ½ c snow peas), brown sauce (1 T, ½ oz), and steamed brown rice (½ c)
- Roasted halibut (4 oz) over asparagus (8 spears) (tossed with 1 tsp olive oil), topped with red pepper relish (2 T minced red bell pepper, 1 T fresh orange juice, 1 tsp olive oil, and ½ tsp honey), and Near East Wheat Pilaf (½ c, 28 g dry)
- Healthy Choice Meals Sesame Chicken and salad (1 c) with sunflower seeds (1 T) and Kraft Fat-Free Red Wine Vinegar dressing (2 T)

- Smart Ones Roast Beef Portobello Dinner; Health Valley Vegetable soup, low fat (1 c); mixed greens, shredded carrot, tomato, and cucumber (1 c) with Kraft Fat-Free Red Wine Vinegar dressing (2 T); and wild rice (½ c)
- Lean Cuisine Spa Cuisine Salmon with Basil frozen entree and Health Valley Fat-Free Tomato Vegetable soup (1½ c)
- California Pizza Kitchen Thai Chicken Pizza (2 slices) and spinach salad (1 c) topped with low-fat goat cheese (1 oz), dried pumpkin seeds (1 T), and dried cherries (1 T) with balsamic vinegar (1 T)

Snacks

The "A," "B," and "C" snacks are antiaging snacks (fruits and vegetables rich in antioxidants, including beta-carotene, vitamin C, and vitamin E); bone-building snacks (containing a quarter of your daily calcium needs); and comfort snacks (sweet or salty "indulgent" treats, including cookies, sweets, and candy).

ANTIAGING ("A") SNACKS. Each antiaging snack contains about 100 calories. Pick one "A" snack each day.

- Cantaloupe (1½ c cubes)
- Medium Red Delicious apple (5 oz) with creamy peanut butter (1 tsp)
- Raw peanuts (1 T) with dried cranberries (½ oz, about 2 T)
- Blueberries (¾ c) with fat-free Cool Whip (1 T) and slivered almonds (1 T)
- Dried apricot halves (5) with walnut halves (5)
- Orange (1 medium, 5 oz) with raw almonds (6)
- Banana (½ medium, 2 oz) with raw almonds (6)
- Sweet cherries (½ c) with pecans (5 halves)
- Strawberries (1 c) with pecans (5 halves)
- Mixed berries (⅓ c blackberries and ¼ c raspberries) with yogurt dressing (3 T) and flaxseeds (1 T)
- Amy's Black Bean and Vegetable soup, low-fat (1 c)

- Prunes (2) with walnut halves (6)
- Crudités of red bell pepper (½ c) and broccoli florets (5) with hummus (3 T)
- Watermelon (1 c cubes) with raw peanuts (1 T)

BONE-BUILDING ("B") SNACKS. "B" snacks contain about 100 calories and at least a quarter of your daily calcium needs (250 mg). Each "B" snack also contains at least 5 grams of protein. Pick one "B" snack each day.

- Starbucks Caffé Latte with fat-free milk (tall, 12 oz)
- La Yogurt Light Nonfat fruit yogurt (6 oz) with All-Bran with Extra Fiber (¼ c)
- Chilled Banana Latte (Mix 1½ T sugar-free crème de banana syrup, 1½ T sugar-free coconut syrup, and 1 c fat-free milk in a 20-oz chilled stainless steel pitcher. Froth milk with whisk until airy and light. Add a shot of espresso and pour over ice.)
- Sargento Light String Cheese Snacks (2)
- Thomas' Light Multigrain English muffin (½) with reduced-fat Swiss cheese (Sargento thin slice) (1 oz)
- Pria bar (110 calories) or any energy bar with 300 mg calcium, 5 g protein, and up to 125 calories
- Blueberry smoothie (Blend 4 oz fat-free milk, 2 oz fat-free blueberry yogurt, ½ c frozen blueberries, and 1 packet of Splenda on high speed until smooth.)
- Vegetable dip (2 T Lipton-Gefen Vegetable Soup & Dip Mix mixed with ½ c fat-free plain yogurt, such as Stonyfield Farm), and baby carrots (¼ c) and red bell pepper strips (¼ c)
- Sugar-free hot cocoa mix (1 packet) made with low-fat milk (8 oz)
- Light n' Lively low-fat cottage cheese with calcium (½ c) with cinnamon (1 tsp) topped with blackberries (½ c)
- Colombo Fat Free Light yogurt (8 oz)
- Cheese kabob: Alternate cubes of low-fat cheddar cheese (2 oz) with cherry tomatoes (3), yellow bell pepper (¼ c), and cucumber (¼ c)

- Starbucks Iced Caffé Latte with soy milk (tall, 12 oz)
- Chocolate milk (8 oz fat-free milk with 1 T Hershey's Lite chocolate syrup)

COMFORT ("C") SNACKS. Each comfort snack contains about 100 calories. Pick one "C" snack each day.

- Hershey's Kisses (4)
- Peanut M&Ms (10)
- Nature Valley Peanut Butter Granola Bar (or another flavor) (1)
- Tootsie Roll Midgees (4)
- Snackwell's vanilla cream cookies (2)
- Animal crackers (20)
- Health Valley Oatmeal Raisin cookie (1)
- Snyder's Organic Honey Wheat Pretzel Sticks (12)
- 98% fat-free vanilla ice cream (such as Breyers) (½ cup)
- Rice Krispies Treat (1)
- Snackwell's bite-size chocolate chip cookies (10)
- Baked tortilla chips (such as Tostitos) (¾ oz, about 15 chips) with salsa (¼ c)
- Nabisco 100-calorie pack (Oreo Thin Crisps; Chips Ahoy Thin Crisps; Honey Maid Cinnamon Thin Crisps; Ritz Snack Mix; Planters Peanut Butter Cookie Crisps)
- Fat-free fudge bar (such as Silhouette) (1)

Week 1 Meal Plan

Day 1

BREAKFAST

Kashi Heart to Heart cereal (1 c) topped with sliced strawberries (1 c), wheat germ (2 tsp), and fat-free milk (1 c)

MIDMORNING "A" SNACK
Cantaloupe (1½ c cubes)

LUNCH
Chicken Greek salad: Grilled chicken breast (2 oz), feta cheese (1½ oz), and black olives (8) over mixed salad greens (1 c) with red onion (⅛ c), cherry tomatoes (5), red bell pepper (¼ c), and cucumber (¼ c) with Kraft Fat-Free Red Wine Vinegar dressing (2 T), and small whole wheat pita (or ½ large)

AFTERNOON "B" SNACK
Light n' Lively low-fat cottage cheese with calcium (½ c) with cinnamon (1 tsp) topped with blackberries (½ c)

DINNER
Lean Cuisine Spa Cuisine Salmon with Basil frozen entree and Health Valley Fat-Free Tomato Vegetable soup (1½ c)

EVENING "C" SNACK
Peanut M&Ms (10)

Day 2

BREAKFAST
Whole wheat toast (1 slice) with creamy peanut butter (1 T), La Yogurt Light Nonfat yogurt (6 oz), and 1 plum

MIDMORNING "B" SNACK
Pria bar (110 calories) or any energy bar with 300 mg calcium, 5 g protein, and up to 125 calories

LUNCH
Tuna (3 oz) with light mayonnaise (2 tsp) on a whole wheat pita with mixed greens, shredded carrot, tomato, and cucumber (1 c) with Annie's Naturals Balsamic Vinaigrette dressing (1 T)

AFTERNOON "A" SNACK
Raw peanuts (1 T) with dried cranberries (½ oz, about 2 T)

DINNER

Turkey fajitas: Turkey breast (4 oz) marinated in lemon
   juice (1½ tsp), rice vinegar (¾ tsp), Worcestershire sauce
   (¾ tsp), salt, black pepper, cumin, crushed coriander
   (¾ tsp), and minced garlic (½ clove) and then sautéed
   (using vegetable oil cooking spray and 1 tsp olive oil)
   with red bell pepper (¼ c), onion (¼ c), carrot (¼ c), and
   tomato (¼ c), served in whole wheat tortilla (6"–8") with
   salsa (2 T) and guacamole (2 T)

EVENING "C" SNACK

Hershey's Kisses (4)

Day 3

BREAKFAST

Whole Grain Total cereal (1 c) with blueberries (¾ c) and
   fat-free milk (1 c)

MIDMORNING "A" SNACK

Medium Red Delicious apple (5 oz) with creamy peanut
   butter (1 tsp)   Smoothie

LUNCH

Thomas' Whole Wheat Sahara Wrap (½) filled with oven-
   roasted turkey breast (3 oz), reduced-fat Swiss cheese
   (Sargento thin slice) (1 slice), romaine lettuce (2 leaves),
   avocado (2 T), slice of tomato, and honey mustard
   (1 T), and mixed greens, shredded carrot, tomato,
   and cucumber (1 c) with Annie's Naturals Balsamic
   Vinaigrette dressing (1 T)

AFTERNOON "B" SNACK

Sugar-free hot cocoa mix (1 packet) made with low-fat milk
   (8 oz)

DINNER *lettuce wraps*

Trout (4 oz) baked with onion (¼ c), bell pepper (½ c),
mushrooms (½ c), diced black olives (4), and stewed
tomatoes (3½ oz) over whole wheat pasta (½ c)

EVENING "C" SNACK

Rice Krispies Treat (1)

Day 4

BREAKFAST

Quaker Oatmeal Nutrition for Women (1 packet) made with
fat-free milk (⅔ c) and topped with raspberries (½ c) and
chopped pecans (1 T)

MIDMORNING "A" SNACK

Dried apricot halves (5) with walnut halves (5)

LUNCH

Chicken salad (3 oz) made with Dijon mustard (2 T)
on whole wheat bread (2 slices), and mixed greens,
shredded carrot, tomato, and cucumber (1 c) with low-fat
dressing (balsamic vinegar) (2 T)

AFTERNOON "B" SNACK

Sargento Light String Cheese Snacks (2)

DINNER

Broiled tilapia fillet (4 oz) seasoned with lemon juice
(1 T), Worcestershire sauce (¼ tsp), and paprika (1 tsp),
medium baked sweet potato (4 oz), and sautéed broccoli
rabe (4 oz, using 2 tsp olive oil)

EVENING "C" SNACK

Snackwell's bite-size chocolate chip cookies (10)

Day 5

BREAKFAST

Thomas' Light Multigrain English muffin (1) with part-skim ricotta (¼ c) and ground cinnamon sprinkled on top (1 tsp) and fresh blueberries (1 c)

MIDMORNING "B" SNACK

Starbucks Caffé Latte with fat-free milk (tall, 12 oz)

LUNCH

Shrimp salad: Large shrimp (10, 2 oz) with blue (or other crumbled) cheese (1 oz) on mixed greens, shredded carrot, tomato, and cucumber (1 c) with peas (¼ c) and Newman's Own Light Raspberry & Walnut Vinaigrette (2 T), and small whole wheat roll (1½ oz)

AFTERNOON "A" SNACK

Amy's Black Bean and Vegetable soup, low-fat (1 c)

DINNER

Healthy Choice Meals Sesame Chicken and salad (1 c) with sunflower seeds (1 T) and Kraft Fat-Free Red Wine Vinegar dressing (2 T)

EVENING "C" SNACK

Nature Valley Peanut Butter Granola Bar (or another flavor) (1)

Day 6

BREAKFAST

Kashi Go Lean cereal (1 c) with Colombo Fat Free Light yogurt (8 oz) and cranberries (1 c)

MIDMORNING "B" SNACK

Thomas' Light Multigrain English muffin (½) with reduced-fat Swiss cheese (Sargento thin slice) (1 oz)

LUNCH

Lean Cuisine Spa Cuisine Chicken in Peanut Sauce frozen
entree and baby spinach salad (1 c) with red onion (⅛ c),
cherry tomatoes (5), red bell pepper (¼ c), yellow bell
pepper (¼ c), cucumber (¼ c), and raw peanuts (1 T)
with Kraft Fat-Free Red Wine Vinegar dressing (2 T)

AFTERNOON "C" SNACK

Snackwell's vanilla cream cookies (2)

DINNER

Broiled salmon fillet (4 oz) with light mayonnaise (1 tsp)
and Dijon mustard (1 T), wild rice (½ c), and steamed
zucchini and squash (1 c)

EVENING "A" SNACK

Blueberries (¾ c) with fat-free Cool Whip (1 T) and slivered
almonds (1 T)

Day 7

BREAKFAST

Low-fat bran muffin (½) with Dannon Light 'n Fit yogurt
(6 oz) and blackberries (1 c)

MIDMORNING "A" SNACK

Sweet cherries (½ c) with pecans (5 halves)

LUNCH

Whole wheat pita filled with hummus (⅓ c), reduced-fat
Swiss cheese (Sargento thin slice) (1 oz), avocado (1 T),
chopped arugula (½ c), tomato (2 slices), chopped carrot
(¼ c), and sprouts (½ c)

AFTERNOON "B" SNACK

Vegetable dip (2 T Lipton-Gefen Vegetable Soup & Dip Mix
mixed with ½ c fat-free plain yogurt, such as Stonyfield
Farm), and baby carrots (¼ c) and red bell pepper strips
(¼ c)

DINNER

Grilled chicken breast (4 oz), sautéed broccoli (1 c, using
  1 tsp olive oil, 2 T dry white wine, ½ clove garlic, 2 tsp
  golden raisins, and red pepper flakes), and couscous
  (½ c)

EVENING "C" SNACK

Nabisco 100-calorie pack (Oreo Thin Crisps; Chips Ahoy
  Thin Crisps; Honey Maid Cinnamon Thin Crisps; Ritz
  Snack Mix; Planters Peanut Butter Cookie Crisps)

AVERAGES FOR THE WEEK*

1,415 calories
50% carbohydrate (31 grams of fiber)
25% protein
25% fat (6% saturated)
1,324 milligrams of calcium

Week 2 Meal Plan

Day 8

BREAKFAST

Spinach omelet (4 egg whites, ½ cup cooked spinach, and
  ½ oz low-fat cheddar cheese), whole wheat toast (1 slice),
  and medium Red Delicious or Gala apple

MIDMORNING "A" SNACK

Strawberries (1 c) with pecans (5 halves)

LUNCH

Oven-roasted turkey breast (3 oz) on whole wheat bread
  (2 slices) with low-fat Muenster cheese (1 oz), spinach
  leaves (2), tomato (2 slices), and honey mustard (1 T)

---

*Calculated using The Food Processor software, ESHA Research,
Salem, Oregon

AFTERNOON "B" SNACK

Chilled Banana Latte (Mix 1½ T sugar-free crème de
banana syrup, 1½ T sugar-free coconut syrup, and 1 c
fat-free milk in a 20-oz chilled stainless steel pitcher.
Froth milk with whisk until airy and light. Add a shot of
espresso and pour over ice.)

DINNER

California Pizza Kitchen Thai Chicken Pizza (2 slices) and
spinach salad (1 c) topped with low-fat goat cheese (1 oz),
dried pumpkin seeds (1 T), and dried cherries (1 T) with
balsamic vinegar (1 T)

EVENING "C" SNACK

Snyder's Organic Honey Wheat Pretzel Sticks (12)

Day 9

BREAKFAST

Kellogg's Complete Bran Flakes (¾ c) and Fiber One (½ c)
topped with raspberries (¾ c) and fat-free milk (1 c)

MIDMORNING "B" SNACK

Starbucks Iced Caffé Latte with soy milk (tall, 12 oz)

LUNCH

Garden vegetable burger (Morningstar Farms) with low-
fat Muenster cheese (1-oz slice) and slice of tomato on
whole wheat bun (1½ oz), and Health Valley 14 Garden
Vegetable soup, fat-free (1 c)

AFTERNOON "A" SNACK

Crudités of red bell pepper (½ c) and broccoli florets (5)
with hummus (3 T)

DINNER

Chinese takeout: Steamed chicken breast (3 oz) with
steamed veggies (1 c mix broccoli, carrots, and water

chestnuts and ½ c snow peas), brown sauce (1 T, ½ oz), and steamed brown rice (½ c)

EVENING "C" SNACK
Animal crackers (20)

Day 10

BREAKFAST
Whole wheat bagel (such as Thomas') (½) with Laughing Cow Light Swiss cheese spread (2 wedges), medium Red Delicious or Gala apple, and fat-free milk (4 oz)

MIDMORNING "B" SNACK
Colombo Fat Free Light yogurt (8 oz)

LUNCH
Poached salmon (3 oz) with light mayonnaise (2 tsp) and dill (1 tsp) over spinach salad (1 c) with red onion (⅛ c), cherry tomatoes (5), red bell pepper (¼ c), and mandarin oranges (¼ c) with Kraft Fat-Free Red Wine Vinegar dressing (2 T), and small whole wheat roll (1½ oz)

AFTERNOON "A" SNACK
Orange (1 medium, 5 oz) with raw almonds (6)

DINNER
Honey mustard chicken (4 oz) (marinate chicken in 2 tsp Dijon mustard, 1¼ tsp honey, and 1½ tsp reduced-sodium soy sauce), wild rice (½ c), and steamed broccoli and carrots (1½ c)

EVENING "C" SNACK
Fat-free fudge bar (such as Silhouette) (1)

Day 11

BREAKFAST

Whole wheat bagel (such as Thomas') (½) with Philadelphia
Fat Free Garden Vegetable Soft Cream Cheese (2 T) and
lox (2 oz), and mixed berries (½ c blackberries and ½ c
raspberries)

MIDMORNING "A" SNACK

Prunes (2) with walnut halves (6)

LUNCH

Tuna (2 oz) on Thomas' Light Multigrain English muffin (1)
topped with melted reduced-fat Swiss cheese (Sargento
thin slice) (1 oz) and sliced tomato (2), and mixed greens,
shredded carrot, tomato, and cucumber (1 c), raisins
(1 T), and sunflower seeds (1 T) with fat-free raspberry
vinaigrette (2 T)

AFTERNOON "B" SNACK

Chocolate milk (8 oz fat-free milk with 1 T Hershey's Lite
chocolate syrup)

DINNER

Sautéed mixed vegetables (1 c zucchini, ½ c mushrooms,
¼ c water chestnuts, ¼ c green onion, ¼ c corn, 1 clove
garlic, 2 tsp olive oil, and 2 tsp light teriyaki sauce),
grilled shrimp (15), and brown rice (½ c)

EVENING "C" SNACK

Baked tortilla chips (such as Tostitos) (¾ oz, about 10–15
chips) with salsa (¼ c)

Day 12

BREAKFAST

Quaker Oatmeal Squares cereal (¾ c) with sliced
strawberries (1 c) and fat-free milk (1 c)

MIDMORNING "A" SNACK
Watermelon (1 c cubes) with raw peanuts (1 T)

LUNCH
Health Valley 3 Bean Mild Vegetarian Chili (1½ c) topped
   with shredded reduced-fat cheddar cheese (2 T) and
   nonfat sour cream (1 T), mixed greens, shredded carrot,
   tomato, and cucumber (1 c) with Newman's Own Light
   Balsamic Vinaigrette dressing (2 T), and Wasa Rye
   Crispbread (1)

AFTERNOON "B" SNACK
La Yogurt Light Nonfat fruit yogurt (6 oz) with All-Bran
   with Extra Fiber (¼ c)

DINNER
Grilled striped bass (4 oz) covered in mixed dried herbs
   (2 tsp), sautéed spinach (1 c, using 1 tsp olive oil), and
   orzo (½ c, 1½ oz dry) with peas (¼ c)

EVENING "C" SNACK
Health Valley Oatmeal Raisin cookie (1)

Day 13

BREAKFAST
Silk Live! Soy raspberry smoothie with raw almonds (6) and
   1 plum

MIDMORNING "A" SNACK
Banana (½ medium, 2 oz) with raw almonds (6)

LUNCH
Campbell's Chunky Chicken Vegetable soup (1½ c, 12 oz);
   mixed greens, shredded carrot, tomato, and cucumber
   (1 c) topped with Gruyère cheese (½ oz) and grilled
   chicken breast (1 oz) with Kraft Fat-Free Red Wine
   Vinegar dressing (2 T); and small whole wheat roll
   (1½ oz)

AFTERNOON "B" SNACK
Cheese kabob: Alternate cubes of low-fat cheddar cheese
(2 oz) with cherry tomatoes (3), yellow bell pepper (¼ c),
and cucumber (¼ c)

DINNER
Smart Ones Roast Beef Portobello Dinner; Health Valley
Vegetable soup, low fat (1 c); mixed greens, shredded
carrot, tomato, and cucumber (1 c) with Kraft Fat-Free
Red Wine Vinegar dressing (2 T); and wild rice (½ c)

EVENING "C" SNACK
98% fat-free vanilla ice cream (such as Breyers) (½ cup)

Day 14

BREAKFAST
Kashi Go Lean waffle (1) spread with low-fat cottage cheese
with calcium (Light n' Lively) (½ c) and low-sugar jelly (1
T), and strawberries (1 c) with fat-free milk (4 oz)

MIDMORNING "B" SNACK
Blueberry smoothie (Blend 4 oz fat-free milk, 2 oz fat-free
blueberry yogurt, ½ c frozen blueberries and 1 packet of
Splenda on high speed until smooth.)

LUNCH
Tuna maki (6 pieces), yellowtail sashimi (1 oz), salmon
sashimi (1 oz), and edamame (½ c not in pod) with
wasabi (1 tsp) and pickled ginger (2 T), and mixed
greens, shredded carrot, tomato, and cucumber (1 c)
with Annie's Naturals Low-Fat Gingerly Vinaigrette
dressing (1 T)

AFTERNOON "A" SNACK
Mixed berries (⅓ c blackberries and ¼ c raspberries) with
yogurt dressing (3 T) and flaxseeds (1 T)

DINNER

Roasted halibut (4 oz) over asparagus (8 spears) (tossed
   with 1 tsp olive oil), topped with red pepper relish (2 T
   minced red bell pepper, 1 T fresh orange juice, 1 tsp
   olive oil, and ½ tsp honey), and Near East Wheat Pilaf
   (½ c, 28 g dry)

EVENING "C" SNACK

Tootsie Roll Midgees (4)

AVERAGES FOR THE WEEK*

1,411 calories
54% carbohydrate (37 grams of fiber)
26% protein
20% fat (5% saturated)
1,167 milligrams of calcium

Shopping List for 1,400-Calorie Meal Plan

FRUITS

Strawberries
Blueberries
Raspberries
Blackberries
Fresh whole cranberries
Red Delicious or Gala apples (medium)
Plums
Avocado
Cantaloupe
Oranges
Bananas

---

*Calculated using The Food Processor software, ESHA Research,
Salem, Oregon

Sweet cherries
Watermelon
Dried cranberries
Dried apricot halves
Raisins (black and golden)
Dried cherries
Prunes

VEGETABLES
Asparagus
Baby spinach
Mixed salad greens
Red onion
Cherry tomatoes
Tomatoes
Yellow bell peppers
Red bell peppers
Carrots (whole, shredded, and baby)
Cucumber
Spinach
Romaine lettuce leaves
Arugula
Sprouts
Squash and zucchini
Broccoli
Mushrooms
Water chestnuts
Green onions
Sweet potatoes (medium)
Broccoli rabe
Garlic

BREADS, GRAINS, AND CEREALS
Kashi Heart to Heart cereal
Kashi Go Lean cereal
Whole Grain Total cereal
Kellogg's Complete Bran Flakes

Quaker Oatmeal Squares cereal

Fiber One cereal

All-Bran with Extra Fiber cereal

Quaker Oatmeal Nutrition for Women

Thomas' Light Multigrain English muffin

Low-fat bran muffin

Kashi Go Lean waffle

Thomas' whole wheat bagel

Wheat germ

Whole wheat pita (small and large)

Small whole wheat rolls (about 1½ oz each)

Thomas' Whole Wheat Sahara Wraps (or similar whole
    wheat wrap)

Wasa Rye Crispbread

Whole wheat bun

Whole wheat tortilla

Stroehmann 100% whole wheat bread (3 g fiber, 70–90
    calories per slice)

Wild rice

Couscous

Brown rice

Orzo

Whole wheat pasta

Near East Wheat Pilaf

Flaxseeds

DAIRY PRODUCTS (MILK, CHEESE, EGGS)

Fat-free milk

Low-fat (1%) milk

La Yogurt Light Nonfat, Dannon Light 'n Fit, or Colombo Fat
    Free Light yogurt

Fat-free blueberry yogurt

Stonyfield Farm fat-free plain yogurt

Stonyfield Farm or Dannon low-fat plain yogurt

Silk Live! Soy smoothie in raspberry

Part-skim ricotta cheese

Eggs (use only egg whites)
Low-fat cheddar cheese (shredded and whole)
Light 'n Lively low-fat cottage cheese with calcium
Laughing Cow Light Swiss cheese spread (wedges)
Philadelphia Fat-Free Garden Vegetable Soft Cream Cheese
Blue cheese (or other crumbled cheese)
Low-fat Muenster cheese
Sargento thin slice reduced-fat Swiss cheese
Feta cheese
Gruyère cheese
Low-fat goat cheese
Sargento Light String Cheese Snacks
Nonfat sour cream

MEAT, FISH, POULTRY
Lox
Canned tuna fish in water
Chicken breasts (skinless)
Large shrimp
Oven-roasted turkey breast
Salmon fillets (wild, Alaskan)
Striped bass fillet
Tilapia fillet
Halibut fillet (Alaskan or Pacific)
Trout fillet

SUSHI
Tuna maki
Yellowtail sashimi
Salmon sashimi

FROZEN FOODS
Frozen blueberries
Morningstar Farms garden vegetable burgers
Lean Cuisine Spa Cuisine Chicken in Peanut Sauce
Lean Cuisine Spa Cuisine Salmon with Basil
Healthy Choice Meals Sesame Chicken

Smart Ones Roast Beef Portobello Dinner
California Pizza Kitchen Thai Chicken Pizza
Fat-free Cool Whip

CANNED AND PACKAGED GOODS
Health Valley 14 Garden Vegetable soup, fat-free
Health Valley 3 Bean Mild Vegetarian Chili
Health Valley Vegetable soup, low-fat
Health Valley Fat-Free Tomato Vegetable soup
Campbell's Chunky Chicken Noodle soup
Campbell's Chunky Chicken Vegetable soup
Amy's Low-Fat Black Bean and Vegetable soup
Mandarin oranges
Stewed tomatoes (3½-oz can)
Salsa
Canned beets
Canned corn
Canned peas
Lipton-Gefen Vegetable Soup & Dip Mix
Sugar-free hot cocoa packets

SNACKS
Hershey's Kisses
Peanut M&Ms
Nature Valley Granola Bars
Rice Krispies Treats
Tootsie Roll Midgees
Animal crackers
Nabisco 100-calorie packs
Snackwell's bite-size chocolate chip cookies
Snackwell's vanilla cream cookies
Health Valley Oatmeal Raisin cookies
Snyder's Organic Honey Wheat Pretzel Sticks
Tostitos baked tortilla chips
Breyers 98% fat-free vanilla ice cream
Silhouette fat-free fudge bars

FATS AND OILS
Olive oil
Pam cooking spray
Creamy peanut butter
Raw peanuts
Sunflower seeds
Chopped pecans
Pecan halves
Slivered almonds
Raw almonds
Walnut halves
Dried pumpkin seeds
Black olives

SALAD DRESSINGS
Kraft Fat-Free Red Wine Vinegar
Annie's Naturals Low-Fat Raspberry Vinaigrette
Annie's Naturals Balsamic Vinaigrette
Annie's Naturals Low-Fat Gingerly Vinaigrette
Newman's Own Light Raspberry & Walnut Vinaigrette
Newman's Own Light Balsamic Vinaigrette

CONDIMENTS
Low-sugar jelly
Light mayonnaise
Lemon juice
Rice vinegar
Worcestershire sauce
Brown sauce
Guacamole
Dijon mustard
Honey mustard
Light teriyaki sauce
Honey
Low-sodium soy sauce
Balsamic vinegar

Wasabi
Pickled ginger

HERBS AND SPICES
Salt
Black pepper
Dill
Cumin
Crushed coriander
Paprika
Ground cinnamon
Red pepper flakes
Dried herbs (e.g., basil, oregano)

MISCELLANEOUS
Pria 110 Plus energy bar (up to 125 calories, 300 mg calcium,
    5 g protein)
Espresso
Hummus
Splenda packets
Dry white wine (for cooking)
Dry-roasted edamame
Hershey's Lite chocolate syrup
Sugar-free crème de banana syrup
Sugar-free coconut syrup

The 1,600-Calorie Meal Plan

8

T he 1,600-calorie plan is appropriate if you are currently exercising at least three times per week, for a minimum of 30 minutes each session, or if you intend to do so. As with the 1,200- and 1,400-calorie plans, I've given you two ways to go about your meals and snacks: You can choose breakfast, lunch, dinner, and snack options from the lists in the first part of this chapter, or you can turn to the chapter's complete two-week meal plan. The options format works well if you want to have total flexibility in what you eat each day, whereas the meal plan format is more structured.

If you find that you are not losing weight on 1,600 calories a day, or you've hit a plateau, I recommend increasing the amount or intensity of your exercise, or dropping back to the 1,400-calorie plan. Remember, if you cut back on calories, 1,200 is the lowest level you should consume. Alternatively, if you find that you are uncomfortably hungry on 1,600 calories, you may double up on your "A" or "B" snacks.

Please note that while brand names are cited frequently, they are *only* examples of foods that match the specific nutritional goals. You can feel free to substitute any food that fits the meal structure, as long as the number of calories is the same. See Appendix A for substitution lists.

Options Format

Your breakfasts include one serving of fruit (mostly the "antiaging" fruits, which are loaded with antioxidants) and one bone-building ("B") food. Each breakfast also contains a source of whole grains or other fiber-rich food and has a moderate amount of protein. Lunch and dinner plates can be visualized as one-third protein, one-third vegetables, and one-third grains—these meals contain the three food groups in calorie-controlled portions. Your options for lunch and dinner vary from prepared dishes, vegetarian courses, and frozen meals. "A," "B," and "C" snacks are listed individually after the dinner options.

Choose one selection from each of the six lists each day.

Breakfast

Each breakfast contains about 325 calories. It provides a minimum of 5 grams of fiber and at least 250 milligrams (mg) of calcium, giving you 25 percent of your daily needs. An antioxidant-rich fruit is a part of every breakfast option.

- Kashi Heart to Heart cereal (1 c) topped with sliced strawberries (1 c), wheat germ (2 tsp), and low-fat (1%) milk (1 c)
- Whole wheat toast (1 slice) with creamy peanut butter (1 T), La Yogurt Light Nonfat yogurt (6 oz), and 1 plum
- Whole Grain Total cereal (1¼ c) with raspberries (¾ c) and low-fat (1%) milk (1 c)
- Quaker Oatmeal Nutrition for Women (1 packet) made with fat-free milk (⅔ c) and topped with blueberries (¾ c) and chopped pecans (1 T)
- Thomas' Light Multigrain English muffin (1) with part-skim ricotta (⅓ cup) and ground cinnamon sprinkled on top (1 tsp) and fresh blueberries (1 c)
- Kashi Go Lean cereal (1 c) with Colombo Fat Free Light yogurt (8 oz) and cranberries (1 c)

- Pria Complete Nutrition Bar with dried apricot halves (8) and raw almonds (12)
- Spinach omelet (4 egg whites, ½ cup cooked spinach, and 1½ oz low-fat cheddar cheese), whole wheat toast (1 slice), and medium Red Delicious or Gala apple
- Kashi Go Lean waffle (2) spread with low-fat cottage cheese with calcium (such as Light n' Lively) (½ c) and strawberries (1 c) with fat-free milk (4 oz)
- Whole wheat bagel (such as Thomas') (½) with Laughing Cow Light Swiss cheese spread (2 wedges), medium Red Delicious or Gala apple, and fat-free milk (4 oz)
- Kellogg's Smart Start Soy Protein (1 c) topped with raspberries (½ c) and fat-free milk (1 c)
- Quaker Oatmeal Squares cereal (¾ c) with sliced strawberries (1 c) and low-fat (1%) milk (1 c)
- Fiber One Honey Clusters cereal (1¼ c) with blackberries (½ c) and low-fat (1%) milk (1 c)
- Whole wheat bagel (such as Thomas') (½) with Philadelphia Fat Free Garden Vegetable Soft Cream Cheese (2 T) and lox (2 oz), and mixed berries (½ c blackberries and ½ c raspberries)

Lunch

Your lunches provide about 450 calories. They also contain a minimum of 6 grams of fiber. Note that each meal comprises approximately one-third each of protein, grains, and vegetables.

- Tuna (4 oz) with light mayonnaise (1 T) on a whole wheat pita with mixed greens, shredded carrot, tomato, and cucumber (1 c) with Annie's Naturals Balsamic Vinaigrette dressing (1 T)
- Chicken salad (4 oz) made with Dijon mustard (2 T) on whole wheat bread (2 slices), and mixed greens, shredded carrot, tomato, and cucumber (1 c) with Newman's Own Light Raspberry & Walnut Vinaigrette (1 T)

- Grilled salmon fillet (3 oz) on mixed greens, shredded carrot, tomato, and cucumber (1 c) with blue (or other crumbled) cheese (1 oz) and Newman's Own Light Raspberry & Walnut Vinaigrette (2 T), and Wasa Rye Crispbread (2)
- Garden vegetable burger (Morningstar Farms) with low-fat Muenster cheese (1-oz slice) and slice of tomato on whole wheat bun (1½ oz), and Amy's Organic Lentil Vegetable soup (1 c)
- Thomas' Whole Wheat Sahara Wrap (1) filled with oven-roasted turkey breast (3 oz), reduced-fat Swiss cheese (Sargento thin slice) (1 oz), romaine lettuce (2 leaves), slice of tomato, and honey mustard (1 T), and mixed greens, shredded carrot, tomato, and cucumber (1 c) with Annie's Naturals Balsamic Vinaigrette dressing (1 T)
- Tuna maki (6 pieces), yellowtail sashimi (2 oz), salmon sashimi (2 oz), and tuna sashimi (1 oz) with wasabi (1 tsp) and pickled ginger (2 T), and mixed greens, shredded carrot, tomato, and cucumber (1 c) with Annie's Naturals Low-Fat Gingerly Vinaigrette dressing (1 T)
- Whole wheat pita filled with hummus (⅓ c), reduced-fat Swiss cheese (Sargento thin slice) (2 oz), chopped arugula (½ c), tomato (2 slices), chopped carrot (¼ c), and sprouts (½ c)
- Poached salmon (4 oz) with light mayonnaise (2 tsp) and dill (1 tsp) over spinach salad (1 c) with red onion (⅛ c), cherry tomatoes (5), red bell pepper (¼ c), and mandarin oranges (¼ c) with Kraft Fat-Free Red Wine Vinegar dressing (2 T), and small whole wheat roll (1½ oz)
- Lean Cuisine Chicken with Almonds and mixed greens, shredded carrot, tomato, and cucumber (1 c), slivered almonds (1 T), and Gruyère cheese (1 oz) with Kraft Fat-Free Red Wine Vinegar dressing (2 T)
- Chicken Greek salad: Grilled chicken breast (3 oz), feta cheese (1½ oz), and black olives (8) over mixed salad greens (1 c) with red onion (⅛ c), cherry tomatoes (5), red bell pepper (¼ c), and cucumber (¼ c) with Kraft Fat-Free Red

Wine Vinegar dressing (2 T), and small whole wheat pita (or ½ large)

- Tuna (4 oz) on Thomas' Light Multigrain English muffin (1) topped with melted reduced-fat Swiss cheese (Sargento thin slice) (1 oz) and sliced tomato (2), and mixed greens, shredded carrot, tomato, and cucumber (1 c), raisins (1 T), and sunflower seeds (1 T) with Kraft Fat-Free Red Wine Vinegar dressing (2 T)
- Oven-roasted turkey breast (3 oz) on whole wheat bread (2 slices) with low-fat Muenster cheese (1 oz), spinach leaves (2), tomato (2 slices), and honey mustard (1 T), and mixed greens, shredded carrot, tomato, and cucumber (1 c) with Annie's Naturals Low-Fat Raspberry Vinaigrette dressing (2 T)
- Campbell's Chunky Chicken Noodle soup (2 c); mixed greens, shredded carrot, tomato, and cucumber (1 c), and grilled chicken breast (1 oz) with Kraft Fat-Free Red Wine Vinegar dressing (2 T); and small whole wheat roll (1½ oz)
- Lean Cuisine Spa Cuisine Chicken in Peanut Sauce frozen entree and baby spinach salad (1 c) with red onion (⅛ c), cherry tomatoes (5), red bell pepper (¼ c), yellow bell pepper (¼ c), cucumber (¼ c), and raw peanuts (1 T) with Annie's Naturals Balsamic Vinaigrette dressing (1 T)

Dinner

Your dinners provide about 450 calories. Each meal is approximately one-third protein, one-third grains, and one-third vegetables.

- Broiled salmon fillet (5 oz) with light mayonnaise (1 tsp) and Dijon mustard (1 T), brown rice (½ c), and steamed zucchini and squash (1 c)
- Grilled chicken breast (4 oz), sautéed broccoli (1½ c, using 1½ tsp olive oil, 2 T dry white wine, ½ clove garlic, 2 tsp golden raisins, and red pepper flakes), and couscous (½ c)
- Sautéed mixed vegetables (1 c zucchini, ½ c mushrooms, ¼ c water chestnuts, ¼ c green onion, ¼ c corn, 1 clove

garlic, 2 tsp olive oil, and 1 T light teriyaki sauce), grilled shrimp (15), and brown rice (¾ c)

- Grilled striped bass (5 oz) covered in mixed dried herbs (2 tsp), sautéed spinach (1 c, using 1 tsp olive oil), and orzo (½ c, 1½ oz dry) with peas (¼ c)
- Honey mustard chicken (4 oz) (marinate chicken in 2 tsp Dijon mustard, 1¼ tsp honey, and 1½ tsp reduced-sodium soy sauce), wild rice (¾ c), and sautéed broccoli and carrots (1½ c, using 1 tsp olive oil)
- Broiled tilapia fillet (4 oz) seasoned with lemon juice (1 T), olive oil (1 tsp), Worcestershire sauce (¼ tsp), and paprika (1 tsp), large baked sweet potato (6 oz), and sautéed broccoli rabe (4 oz, using 2 tsp olive oil)
- Trout (5 oz) baked with onion (¼ c), bell pepper (½ c), mushrooms (½ c), diced black olives (4), and stewed tomatoes (3½ oz) over whole wheat pasta (½ c)
- Turkey fajitas: Turkey breast (4 oz) marinated in lemon juice (1½ tsp), rice vinegar (¾ tsp), Worcestershire sauce (¾ tsp), salt, black pepper, cumin, crushed coriander (¾ tsp), and minced garlic (½ clove) and then sautéed (using 2 tsp olive oil) with red bell pepper (¼ c), onion (¼ c), carrot (¼ c), and tomato (¼ c), served in whole wheat tortilla (6″–8″) with salsa (¼ c) and guacamole (2 T)
- Chinese takeout: Steamed chicken breast (4 oz) with sautéed veggies (1 c mix broccoli, carrots, and water chestnuts and ½ c snow peas, using 1 tsp olive oil), brown sauce (1 T, ½ oz), and steamed brown rice (½ c)
- Roasted halibut (4 oz) over asparagus (10 spears) (tossed with 1 tsp olive oil), topped with red pepper relish (2 T minced red pepper, 1 T fresh orange juice, 1 tsp olive oil, and ½ tsp honey), and Near East Wheat Pilaf (¾ c, 42 g dry)
- Healthy Choice Meals Chicken with Roasted Red Pepper Dipping Sauce and mixed greens, shredded carrot, tomato, and cucumber (1 c) with Annie's Naturals Balsamic Vinaigrette dressing (1 T)

- Smart Ones Roast Beef Portobello Dinner; Health Valley Vegetable soup, low-fat (1 c); side salad (1 c) with Newman's Own Light Balsamic Vinaigrette dressing (2 T); and wild rice (½ c)
- Lean Cuisine Spa Cuisine Salmon with Basil frozen entree and Health Valley Low-Fat Lentil soup (1½ c)
- Lean Cuisine Spinach and Mushroom Pizza and spinach salad (1 c) topped with low-fat goat cheese (1 oz), dried pumpkin seeds (1 T), and dried cherries (1 T) with balsamic vinegar (2 T)

Snacks

The "A," "B," and "C" snacks are, respectively, "antiaging" fruits and vegetables rich in antioxidants, including beta-carotene and vitamins C and E; "bone-building" treats containing a quarter of your daily calcium needs; and "comfort" snacks—sweet or salty indulgences along the lines of cookies and candy.

ANTIAGING ("A") SNACKS. Each antiaging snack contains about 125 calories. Pick one "A" snack each day.

- Cantaloupe (1½ c cubes) with sunflower seeds (1 T)
- Large Red Delicious apple (7–8 oz) with creamy peanut butter (1 tsp)
- Raw peanuts (1 T) with dried cranberries (¼ c)
- Blueberries (1 c) with fat-free Cool Whip (1 T) and slivered almonds (1 T)
- Dried apricot halves (5) with walnut halves (6)
- Orange (1 large, 6½ oz) with raw almonds (6)
- Banana (1 medium, 4 oz) with raw almonds (6)
- Sweet cherries (1 c) with pecans (5 halves)
- Strawberries (1 c) with pecans (8 halves)
- Mixed berries (½ c blackberries and ½ c raspberries) with yogurt dressing (3 T) and flaxseeds (1 T)

- Health Valley Low-Fat Black Bean soup (1 c)
- Prunes (3) with walnut halves (5)
- Crudités of baby carrots (¼ c), red bell pepper (½ c), and broccoli florets (5) with hummus (¼ c)
- Watermelon (2 c cubes) with raw peanuts (1 T)

BONE-BUILDING ("B") SNACKS. "B" snacks contain about 125 calories and at least a quarter (250 mg) of your daily calcium needs. Each "B" snack also contains at least 5 grams of protein. Pick one each day.

- Starbucks Caffé Latte with fat-free milk (tall, 12 oz)
- Glenny's Low-Fat Soy Crisps, BBQ (1 bag)
- Sargento Light String Cheese Snacks (2) with Wheat Thins (5)
- Thomas' Light Multigrain English muffin (½) with reduced-fat Swiss cheese (Sargento thin slice) (1 oz)
- Pria bar (110 calories) or any energy bar with 300 mg calcium, 5 g protein, and up to 125 calories
- Mixed-berry yogurt smoothie: Blend ½ c low-fat plain yogurt (Dannon) with ½ c strawberries, ½ c raspberries, and ice on high speed until smooth
- Vegetable dip (2 T Lipton-Gefen Vegetable Soup & Dip Mix mixed with ½ c low-fat plain yogurt) with baby carrots (¼ c) and red bell pepper strips (½ c)
- Sugar-free hot cocoa mix (1 packet) made with low-fat milk (8 oz)
- Light n' Lively low-fat cottage cheese with calcium (½ c) topped with blackberries (½ c) and slivered almonds (2 tsp)
- Stonyfield Farm Organic Low-Fat Yogurt Smoothie (6-oz bottle)
- Stonyfield Farm low-fat flavored yogurt (6 oz)
- Cheese kabob: Alternate cubes of low-fat cheddar cheese (2 oz) with cherry tomatoes (3), yellow bell pepper (¼ c), and cucumber (¼ c)

Check Out Receipt

Dyer-Schererville Branch
219-322-4731

Tuesday, November 1, 2016 3:44:49 PM
11626
DONALDSON, PATRICIA A

Item: 33113025816853
Title: Strong, slim, and 30! : eat right,
stay young, feel great, and look fabulous
Call no.: 613.2082 DRAY
Due: 11/15/2016

Total items: 1

Thank You!

- Starbucks Iced Caffé Latte made with low-fat milk (grande, 16 oz)
- Silk Soy Milk—Very Vanilla (8¼ oz)

COMFORT ("C") SNACKS. Each comfort snack contains about 125 calories. Pick one "C" snack each day.

- Hershey's Kisses (5)
- Peanut M&Ms (12)
- Nabisco Honey Maid Cinnamon Graham Crackers (2 sheets/ 8 crackers)
- Tootsie Roll Midgees (5)
- Pepperidge Farm Hazelnut Pirouette cookies (2)
- Animal crackers (20)
- Health Valley Low-Fat Amaretto Biscotti Style cookies (2)
- Snyder's Organic Honey Wheat Pretzel Sticks (1 oz, 15 sticks)
- Light vanilla ice cream (50% less fat) (½ c)
- Baked tortilla chips (such as Tostitos) (1 oz, about 20) with salsa (¼ c, 2 oz)
- Snackwell's bite-size chocolate chip cookies (13)
- Health Valley Moist and Chewy Peanut Crunch Granola Bar (1)
- Nabisco 100-calorie pack (Oreo Thin Crisps; Chips Ahoy Thin Crisps; Honey Maid Cinnamon Thin Crisps; Ritz Snack Mix; Planters Peanut Butter Cookie Crisps)
- Chocolate or vanilla ice cream sandwich (98% fat-free, such as Silhouette) (1)

Week 1 Meal Plan

Day 1

BREAKFAST
Kashi Heart to Heart cereal (1 c) topped with sliced strawberries (1 c), wheat germ (2 tsp), and low-fat (1%) milk (1 c)

MIDMORNING "A" SNACK
Banana (1 medium, 4 oz) with raw almonds (6)

LUNCH
Poached salmon (4 oz) mixed with light mayonnaise (2 tsp) and dill (1 tsp) over spinach salad (1 c) with red onion (⅛ c), cherry tomatoes (5), red bell pepper (¼ c), and mandarin oranges (¼ c) with Kraft Fat-Free Red Wine Vinegar dressing (2 T), and small whole wheat roll (1½ oz)

AFTERNOON "B" SNACK
Pria bar (110 calories) or any energy bar with 300 mg calcium, 5 g protein, and up to 125 calories

DINNER
Turkey fajitas: Turkey breast (4 oz) marinated in lemon juice (1½ tsp), rice vinegar (¾ tsp), Worcestershire sauce (¾ tsp), salt, black pepper, cumin, crushed coriander (¾ tsp), and minced garlic (½ clove) and then sautéed (using 2 tsp olive oil) with red bell pepper (¼ c), onion (¼ c), carrot (¼ c), and tomato (¼ c), served in whole wheat tortilla (6"–8") with salsa (¼ c) and guacamole (2 T)

EVENING "C" SNACK
Pepperidge Farm Hazelnut Pirouette cookies (2)

Day 2

BREAKFAST

Whole wheat toast (1 slice) with creamy peanut butter (1 T), La Yogurt Light Nonfat yogurt (6 oz), and 1 plum

MIDMORNING "B" SNACK

Mixed-berry yogurt smoothie: Blend ½ c low-fat plain yogurt (Dannon) with ½ c strawberries, ½ c raspberries, and ice on high speed until smooth

LUNCH

Campbell's Chunky Chicken Noodle soup (2 c), with mixed greens, shredded carrot, tomato, and cucumber (1 c), and grilled chicken breast (1 oz) with Kraft Fat-Free Red Wine Vinegar dressing (2 T), and small whole wheat roll (1½ oz)

AFTERNOON "A" SNACK

Cantaloupe (1½ c cubes) with sunflower seeds (1 T)

DINNER

Broiled tilapia fillet (4 oz) seasoned with lemon juice (1 T), olive oil (1 tsp), Worcestershire sauce (¼ tsp), and paprika (1 tsp), large baked sweet potato (6 oz), and sautéed broccoli rabe (4 oz, using 2 tsp olive oil)

EVENING "C" SNACK

Baked tortilla chips (such as Tostitos) (1 oz, about 20) with salsa (¼ c, 2 oz)

Day 3

BREAKFAST

Whole Grain Total cereal (1¼ c) with raspberries (¾ c) and low-fat (1%) milk (1 c)

MIDMORNING "A" SNACK

Prunes (3) with walnut halves (5)

LUNCH

Oven-roasted turkey breast (3 oz) on whole wheat bread
(2 slices) with low-fat Muenster cheese (1 oz), spinach
leaves (2), tomato (2 slices), and honey mustard (1 T),
and mixed greens, shredded carrot, tomato, and
cucumber (1 c) with Annie's Naturals Low-Fat Raspberry
Vinaigrette dressing (2 T)

AFTERNOON "B" SNACK

Light n' Lively low-fat cottage cheese with calcium (½ c)
topped with blackberries (½ c) and slivered almonds
(2 tsp)

DINNER

Broiled salmon fillet (5 oz) with light mayonnaise (1 tsp)
and Dijon mustard (1 T), brown rice (½ c), and steamed
zucchini and squash (1 c)

EVENING "C" SNACK

Chocolate or vanilla ice cream sandwich (98% fat-free, such
as Silhouette) (1)

Day 4

BREAKFAST

Whole wheat bagel (such as Thomas') (½) with Laughing
Cow Light Swiss cheese spread (2 wedges), medium Red
Delicious or Gala apple, and fat-free milk (4 oz)

MIDMORNING "B" SNACK

Stonyfield Farm Organic Low-Fat Yogurt Smoothie (6-oz
bottle)

LUNCH

Chicken Greek salad: Grilled chicken breast (3 oz), feta
cheese (1½ oz), and black olives (8) over mixed salad
greens (1 c) with red onion (⅛ c), cherry tomatoes (5),
red bell pepper (¼ c), and cucumber (¼ c) with Kraft

Fat-Free Red Wine Vinegar dressing (2 T), and small whole wheat pita (or ½ large)

AFTERNOON "A" SNACK

Raw peanuts (1 T) with dried cranberries (¼ c)

DINNER

Lean Cuisine Spinach and Mushroom Pizza and spinach salad (1 c) topped with low-fat goat cheese (1 oz), dried pumpkin seeds (1 T), and dried cherries (1 T) with balsamic vinegar (2 T)

EVENING "C" SNACK

Health Valley Moist and Chewy Peanut Crunch Granola Bar (1)

Day 5

BREAKFAST

Quaker Oatmeal Nutrition for Women (1 packet) made with fat-free milk (⅔ c) and topped with blueberries (¾ c) and chopped pecans (1 T)

MIDMORNING "A" SNACK

Dried apricot halves (5) with walnut halves (6)

LUNCH

Tuna maki (6 pieces), yellowtail sashimi (2 oz), salmon sashimi (2 oz), and tuna sashimi (1 oz) with wasabi (1 tsp) and pickled ginger (2 T), and mixed greens, shredded carrot, tomato, and cucumber (1 c) with Annie's Naturals Low-Fat Gingerly Vinaigrette dressing (1 T)

AFTERNOON "B" SNACK

Stonyfield Farm low-fat flavored yogurt (6 oz)

DINNER

Smart Ones Roast Beef Portobello Dinner; Health Valley Vegetable soup, low-fat (1 c); mixed greens, shredded

carrot, tomato, and cucumber (1 c) with Newman's Own
Light Balsamic Vinaigrette dressing (2 T); and wild rice
(½ c)

EVENING "C" SNACK
Nabisco 100-calorie pack (Oreo Thin Crisps; Chips Ahoy
Thin Crisps; Honey Maid Cinnamon Thin Crisps; Ritz
Snack Mix; Planters Peanut Butter Cookie Crisps)

Day 6

BREAKFAST
Thomas' Light Multigrain English muffin (1) with part-skim
ricotta (⅓ cup) and ground cinnamon sprinkled on top
(1 tsp) and fresh blueberries (1 c)

MIDMORNING "B" SNACK
Sargento Light String Cheese Snacks (2) with Wheat Thins
(5)

LUNCH
Garden vegetable burger (Morningstar Farms) with low-fat
Muenster cheese (1-oz slice) and slice of tomato on whole
wheat bun (1½ oz), and Amy's Organic Lentil Vegetable
soup (1 c)

AFTERNOON "A" SNACK
Orange (1 large, 6½ oz) with raw almonds (6)

DINNER
Grilled striped bass (5 oz) covered in mixed dried herbs
(2 tsp), sautéed spinach (1 c, using 1 tsp olive oil), and
orzo (½ c, 1½ oz dry) with peas (¼ c)

EVENING "C" SNACK
Tootsie Roll Midgees (5)

Day 7

BREAKFAST

Kashi Go Lean cereal (1 c) with Colombo Fat Free Light
   yogurt (8 oz) and cranberries (1 c)

MIDMORNING "B" SNACK

Silk Soy Milk—Very Vanilla (8¼ oz)

LUNCH

Lean Cuisine Spa Cuisine Chicken in Peanut Sauce frozen
   entree and baby spinach salad (1 c) with red onion (⅛ c),
   cherry tomatoes (5), red bell pepper (¼ c), yellow bell
   pepper (¼ c), cucumber (¼ c), and raw peanuts (1 T)
   with Annie's Naturals Balsamic Vinaigrette dressing
   (1 T)

AFTERNOON "A" SNACK

Crudités of baby carrots (¼ c), red bell pepper strips (½ c),
   and broccoli florets (5) with hummus (¼ c)

DINNER

Trout (5 oz) baked with onion (¼ c), bell pepper (½ c),
   mushrooms (½ c), diced black olives (4), and stewed
   tomatoes (3½ oz) over whole wheat pasta (½ c)

EVENING "C" SNACK

Hershey's Kisses (5)

AVERAGES FOR THE WEEK*

1,611 calories
51% carbohydrate (33 grams of fiber)
24% protein
25% fat (7% saturated)
1,392 milligrams of calcium

---

*Calculated using The Food Processor software, ESHA Research,
 Salem, Oregon

Week 2 Meal Plan

Day 8

BREAKFAST

Pria Complete Nutrition Bar with dried apricot halves (8) and raw almonds (12)

MIDMORNING "B" SNACK

Starbucks Iced Caffé Latte made with low-fat milk (grande, 16 oz)

LUNCH

Chicken salad (4 oz) made with Dijon mustard (2 T) on whole wheat bread (2 slices), and mixed greens, shredded carrot, tomato, and cucumber (1 c) with Newman's Own Light Raspberry & Walnut Vinaigrette (1 T)

AFTERNOON "C" SNACK

Snyder's Organic Honey Wheat Pretzel Sticks (1 oz, 15 sticks)

DINNER

Sautéed mixed vegetables (1 c zucchini, ½ c mushrooms, ¼ c water chestnuts, ¼ c green onion, ¼ c corn, 1 clove garlic, 2 tsp olive oil, and 1 T light teriyaki sauce), grilled shrimp (15), and brown rice (¾ c)

EVENING "A" SNACK

Strawberries (1 c) with pecans (8 halves)

Day 9

BREAKFAST

Spinach omelet (4 egg whites, ½ cup cooked spinach, and 1½ oz low-fat cheddar cheese), whole wheat toast (1 slice), and medium Red Delicious or Gala apple

MIDMORNING "B" SNACK

Sugar-free hot cocoa mix (1 packet) made with low-fat milk (8 oz)

LUNCH

Tuna (4 oz) with light mayonnaise (1 T) on a whole wheat pita with mixed greens, shredded carrot, tomato, and cucumber (1 c) with Annie's Naturals Balsamic Vinaigrette dressing (1 T)

AFTERNOON "C" SNACK

Animal crackers (20)

DINNER

Healthy Choice Meals Chicken with Roasted Red Pepper Dipping Sauce and side salad (1 c) with Annie's Naturals Balsamic Vinaigrette dressing (1 T)

EVENING "A" SNACK

Blueberries (1 c) with fat-free Cool whip (1 T) and slivered almonds (1 T)

Day 10

BREAKFAST

Kashi Go Lean waffle (2) spread with low-fat cottage cheese with calcium (such as Light n' Lively) (½ c) and strawberries (1 c) with fat-free milk (4 oz)

MIDMORNING "A" SNACK

Large Red Delicious apple (7–8 oz) with creamy peanut butter (1 tsp)

LUNCH

Whole wheat pita filled with hummus (⅓ c), reduced-fat Swiss cheese (Sargento thin slice) (2 oz), chopped arugula (½ c), tomato (2 slices), chopped carrot (¼ c), and sprouts (½ c)

AFTERNOON "B" SNACK

Cheese kabob: Alternate cubes of low-fat cheddar cheese
(2 oz) with cherry tomatoes (3), yellow bell pepper (¼ c),
and cucumber (¼ c)

DINNER

Roasted halibut (4 oz) over asparagus (10 spears) (tossed
with 1 tsp olive oil), topped with red pepper relish (2 T
minced red bell pepper, 1 T fresh orange juice, 1 tsp
olive oil, and ½ tsp honey), and Near East Wheat Pilaf
(¼ c, 42 g dry)

EVENING "C" SNACK

Light vanilla ice cream (50% less fat) (½ c)

Day 11

BREAKFAST

Kellogg's Smart Start Soy Protein (1 c) topped with
raspberries (½ c) and fat-free milk (1 c)

MIDMORNING "A" SNACK

Sweet cherries (1 c) with pecans (5 halves)

LUNCH

Thomas' Whole Wheat Sahara Wrap (1) filled with oven-
roasted turkey breast (3 oz), reduced-fat Swiss cheese
(Sargento thin slice) (1 oz), romaine lettuce (2 leaves),
slice of tomato, and honey mustard (1 T), and mixed
greens, shredded carrot, tomato, and cucumber (1 c)
with Annie's Naturals Balsamic Vinaigrette dressing
(1 T)

AFTERNOON "B" SNACK

Thomas' Light Multigrain English muffin (½) with reduced-
fat Swiss cheese (Sargento thin slice) (1 oz)

DINNER

Honey mustard chicken (4 oz) (marinate chicken in 2 tsp
Dijon mustard, 1¼ tsp honey, and 1½ tsp reduced-
sodium soy sauce), wild rice (¾ c), and sautéed broccoli
and carrots (1½ c, using 1 tsp olive oil)

EVENING "C" SNACK

Peanut M&Ms (12)

Day 12

BREAKFAST

Quaker Oatmeal Squares cereal (¾ c) with sliced
strawberries (1 c) and low-fat (1%) milk (1 c)

MIDMORNING "B" SNACK

Starbucks Caffé Latte with fat-free milk (tall, 12 oz)

LUNCH

Lean Cuisine Chicken with Almonds and mixed greens,
shredded carrot, tomato, and cucumber (1 c), slivered
almonds (1 T), and Gruyère cheese (1 oz) with Kraft Fat-
Free Red Wine Vinegar dressing (2 T)

AFTERNOON "A" SNACK

Mixed berries (½ c blackberries and ½ c raspberries) with
yogurt dressing (3 T) and flaxseeds (1 T)

DINNER

Grilled chicken breast (4 oz), sautéed broccoli (1½ c, using
1½ tsp olive oil, 2 T dry white wine, ½ clove garlic, 2 tsp
golden raisins, and red pepper flakes), and couscous
(½ c)

EVENING "C" SNACK

Nabisco Honey Maid Cinnamon Graham Crackers
(2 sheets/8 crackers)

Day 13

BREAKFAST

Fiber One Honey Clusters cereal (1¼ c) with blackberries (½ c) and low-fat (1%) milk (1 c)

MIDMORNING "C" SNACK

Health Valley Low-Fat Amaretto Biscotti Style cookies (2)

LUNCH

Grilled salmon fillet (3 oz) on mixed greens, shredded carrot, tomato, and cucumber (1 c) with blue (or other crumbled) cheese (1 oz) and Newman's Own Light Raspberry & Walnut Vinaigrette (2 T), and Wasa Rye Crispbread (2)

AFTERNOON "A" SNACK

Health Valley Low-Fat Black Bean soup (1 c)

DINNER

Chinese takeout: Steamed chicken breast (4 oz) with sautéed veggies (1 c mix broccoli, carrots, and water chestnuts and ½ c snow peas, using 1 tsp olive oil), brown sauce (1 T, ½ oz), and steamed brown rice (½ c)

EVENING "B" SNACK

Vegetable dip (2 T Lipton-Gefen Vegetable Soup & Dip Mix mixed with ½ c low-fat plain yogurt) with baby carrots (¼ c) and red bell pepper strips (½ c)

Day 14

BREAKFAST

Whole wheat bagel (such as Thomas') (½) with Philadelphia Fat Free Garden Vegetable Soft Cream Cheese (2 T) and lox (2 oz), and mixed berries (½ c blackberries and ½ c raspberries)

MIDMORNING "A" SNACK

Watermelon (2 c cubes) with raw peanuts (1 T)

LUNCH

Tuna (4 oz) on Thomas' Light Multigrain English muffin (1) topped with melted reduced-fat Swiss cheese (Sargento thin slice) (1 oz) and sliced tomato (2), and mixed greens, shredded carrot, tomato, and cucumber (1 c), raisins (1 T), and sunflower seeds (1 T) with Kraft Fat-Free Red Wine Vinegar dressing (2 T)

AFTERNOON "B" SNACK

Glenny's Low-Fat Soy Crisps, BBQ (1 bag)

DINNER

Lean Cuisine Spa Cuisine Salmon with Basil frozen entree and Health Valley Low-Fat Lentil soup (1½ c)

EVENING "C" SNACK

Snackwell's bite-size chocolate chip cookies (13)

AVERAGES FOR THE WEEK*

1,620 calories

50% carbohydrate (37 grams of fiber)

26% protein

24% fat (6% saturated)

1,243 milligrams of calcium

Shopping List for 1,600-Calorie Meal Plan

FRUITS

Strawberries

Blueberries

Raspberries

---

*Calculated using The Food Processor software, ESHA Research, Salem, Oregon

Blackberries
Fresh whole cranberries
Red Delicious or Gala apples (small and medium)
Plums
Cantaloupe
Oranges
Bananas
Sweet cherries
Watermelon
Dried cranberries
Dried apricot halves
Raisins (black and golden)
Dried cherries
Prunes

VEGETABLES
Asparagus
Baby spinach
Mixed salad greens
Red onion
Cherry tomatoes
Tomatoes
Yellow bell peppers
Red bell peppers
Carrots (whole, shredded, and baby)
Cucumber
Spinach
Romaine lettuce leaves
Arugula
Sprouts
Squash and zucchini
Broccoli
Mushrooms
Water chestnuts
Green onions
Sweet potatoes (large)

Broccoli rabe
Garlic

BREADS, GRAINS, AND CEREALS

Kashi Heart to Heart cereal
Kashi Go Lean cereal
Whole Grain Total cereal
Kellogg's Smart Start Soy Protein cereal
Quaker Oatmeal Squares cereal
Fiber One Honey Clusters cereal
Quaker Oatmeal Nutrition for Women
Thomas' Light Multigrain English muffin
Kashi Go Lean waffle
Thomas' whole wheat bagel
Wheat germ
Whole wheat pita (small and large)
Small whole wheat rolls (about 1½ oz each)
Thomas' Whole Wheat Sahara Wraps (or another similar
    whole wheat wrap)
Wasa Rye Crispbread
Whole wheat bun
Whole wheat tortilla
Stroehmann 100% whole wheat bread (3 g fiber, 70–90
    calories per slice)
Wild rice
Couscous
Brown rice
Orzo
Whole wheat pasta
Near East Wheat Pilaf
Flaxseeds
Wheat Thins

DAIRY PRODUCTS (MILK, CHEESE, EGGS)

Fat-free milk
Low-fat (1%) milk
Silk Soy Milk—Very Vanilla (8¼ oz)

La Yogurt Light Nonfat, Dannon Light 'n Fit, or Colombo Fat
   Free Light yogurt
Stonyfield Farm or Dannon low-fat plain yogurt
Stonyfield Farm Organic Low-Fat Yogurt Smoothie
Part-skim ricotta cheese
Eggs (use only egg whites)
Low-fat cheddar cheese (shredded and whole)
Light n' Lively low-fat cottage cheese with calcium
Laughing Cow Light Swiss cheese spread (wedges)
Philadelphia Fat-Free Garden Vegetable Soft Cream Cheese
Blue cheese (or other crumbled cheese)
Low-fat Muenster cheese
Sargento thin slice reduced-fat Swiss cheese
Feta cheese
Gruyère cheese
Low-fat goat cheese
Sargento Light String Cheese Snacks

MEAT, FISH, POULTRY
Lox
Canned tuna fish in water
Chicken breasts (skinless)
Large shrimp
Oven-roasted turkey breast
Salmon fillets (wild, Alaskan)
Striped bass fillet
Tilapia fillet
Halibut fillet (Alaskan or Pacific)
Trout fillet

SUSHI
Tuna maki
Salmon sashimi
Tuna sashimi
Yellowtail sashimi

FROZEN FOODS

Morningstar Farms garden vegetable burgers
Lean Cuisine Spa Cuisine Chicken in Peanut Sauce
Lean Cuisine Spa Cuisine Salmon with Basil
Lean Cuisine Chicken with Almonds
Healthy Choice Meals Chicken with Roasted Red Pepper
  Dipping Sauce
Smart Ones Roast Beef Portobello Dinner
Lean Cuisine Spinach and Mushroom Pizza
Fat-free Cool Whip

CANNED AND PACKAGED GOODS

Health Valley Vegetable soup, low-fat
Health Valley Low-Fat Lentil soup
Health Valley Low-Fat Black Bean soup
Campbell's Chunky Chicken Noodle soup
Amy's Organic Lentil Vegetable soup
Mandarin oranges
Stewed tomatoes (3½-oz can)
Salsa
Canned corn
Canned peas
Lipton-Gefen Vegetable Soup & Dip Mix
Sugar-free hot cocoa packets

SNACKS

Glenny's Low-Fat Soy Crisps, BBQ
Hershey's Kisses
Peanut M&Ms
Tootsie Roll Midgees
Nabisco Honey Maid Cinnamon Graham Crackers
Animal crackers
Nabisco 100-calorie packs
Pepperidge Farm Hazelnut Pirouette cookies
Snackwell's bite-size chocolate chip cookies

Health Valley Low-Fat Amaretto Biscotti Style cookies
Health Valley Moist and Chewy Peanut Crunch Granola Bar
Snyder's Organic Honey Wheat Pretzel Sticks
Tostitos baked tortilla chips
Light vanilla ice cream (50% less fat)
Silhouette 98% fat-free chocolate and vanilla ice cream
    sandwiches

FATS AND OILS

Olive oil
Creamy peanut butter
Raw peanuts
Sunflower seeds
Chopped pecans
Pecan halves
Slivered almonds
Raw almonds
Walnut halves
Dried pumpkin seeds
Black olives

SALAD DRESSINGS

Kraft Fat-Free Red Wine Vinegar
Annie's Naturals Low-Fat Raspberry Vinaigrette
Annie's Naturals Balsamic Vinaigrette
Annie's Naturals Low-Fat Gingerly Vinaigrette
Newman's Own Light Raspberry & Walnut Vinaigrette
Newman's Own Light Balsamic Vinaigrette

CONDIMENTS

Light mayonnaise
Lemon juice
Rice vinegar
Worcestershire sauce
Brown sauce
Guacamole

Dijon mustard
Honey mustard
Light teriyaki sauce
Honey
Low-sodium soy sauce
Balsamic vinegar
Wasabi
Pickled ginger

HERBS AND SPICES
Salt
Black pepper
Dill
Cumin
Crushed coriander
Paprika
Ground cinnamon
Red pepper flakes
Dried herbs (e.g., basil, oregano)

MISCELLANEOUS
Pria 110 Plus energy bar (up to 125 calories, 300 mg calcium,
    5 g protein)
Pria Complete Nutrition energy bar (up to 170 calories; 400
    mg calcium, 11 g protein)
Hummus
Dry white wine (for cooking)

PART 3

Applying the Plan for the Long Term

Preparing for Pregnancy

hen you're in your 20s, you think: I want to look fabulous; I need to stay slim! Right around the time you reach your 30s, however, those thoughts may undergo a shift. New desires may be added to your wish list: I want to look fabulous, yes. But now, I also want to stay healthy. And I want to have a healthy baby—or two or three!

If you're considering starting a family, you'll likely become supermotivated about eating a healthy, balanced diet. Your desire to bear children brings a new meaning to eating well and taking care of yourself—one that differs from fitting into last year's Levi's. No one is saying you've lost your sense of glamour and you're ready for sweats and ponytails every day from here on. Not even close. But your intention to healthfully conceive and deliver a healthy baby may outweigh former goals, at least for the time being.

Talk about multitasking: your prospects for success are excellent, because if you've been following this plan, you're on your way to enhancing your fertility during this prime time in your life. The plan is calorie controlled, allowing you to achieve a healthy body weight prior to pregnancy. This is key. Plus, many of the foods in the plan contain a wide variety of nutrients (such as calcium, iron, and—perhaps most critical—folic acid) that are responsible for vital functions during pregnancy.

Eva's Story

When Eva, now a 38-year-old mother, moved overseas to New York City, she could not find a job and had difficulty adjusting to her new life. "I tend to eat a lot of chocolate and drink a lot of coffee when I'm depressed, or when I just feel lost in a new place. That's how I felt . . . totally detached," she says. The pounds piled up quickly while Eva got accustomed to her new surroundings, and she jumped from a size 6–8 up to a 10, and then to 12. She was concerned about carrying excess weight, because at the time, she and her husband were planning on having their first child. Despite her best intentions—and a neighborhood gym membership—Eva never managed to rid herself of her extra pounds before her pregnancy, and she has continued to struggle with weight issues ever since.

When I first met Eva, she was at a comfortable size 10 and very interested in shedding some pounds while learning how to eat a healthy and varied diet. She told me that within two years, she and her husband wanted to have a second child, but she was apprehensive about being pregnant in her early 40s and having to get back into shape after a second pregnancy. "I hear everywhere that the older you get, the more of a challenge it is; so, I guess my safest bet would be to get in the best possible shape in these upcoming two years," she added.

A professor of college English with two master's degrees, Eva knew a bit about what constitutes a healthy diet, but she wasn't able to put it into action. When we first spoke, she was in such a bad rut, she said, that she couldn't get out of it. Her hectic life, sagging with work and family responsibilities, was overwhelming her.

I assured her that she didn't have to master the plan over-night (in fact, in her case, it would be counterproductive) and encouraged her to set one new goal each week. First we worked on reducing her portions and eating more frequently. Then we gradually added "A", "B," and "C" snacks. Eva fol-lowed my suggestions, and within the first two weeks, she had impressive results to report: "I feel 100 percent better, and I noticed a significant change in my energy level, mood, and general well-being. I never feel hungry, and the portions are just right. I'm sure the balanced meals and snacks—and eating every three to four hours—have contributed to my refreshed new attitude."

Eva faithfully continued on the plan. By the end, she dropped a total of 14 pounds, putting her in perfect preg-nancy shape. Plus, confident that her diet offered balanced nutrition, including many important prepregnancy nutri-ents such as protein, calcium, iron, and folic acid, she felt much better prepared this time around.

Preparing for Pregnancy: A Weighty Issue

Maintaining a healthy body weight is critical for a healthy pregnancy. One recent study published in *Pediatrics* esti-mated that overweight women had twice the risk of having babies born with birth defects and heart abnormalities, com-pared with women who were at a healthy body weight. Being overweight was defined as a body mass index (BMI) of 25 or above—for example, a woman who is 5'4" and weighs 150 pounds. Additionally, obese women (those with a BMI of 30 or above) were shown to have more than *triple* the risk of having babies born with omphalocele, a defect of the intestinal tract.

A couple of theories may explain the links between extra poundage and birth defects. For one, overweight women may not be eating the most healthful foods, leaving their diets devoid of crucial nutrients. Take folic acid, for example. This important B vitamin helps to protect a growing fetus against neural-tube defects such as spina bifida. An overweight woman consuming a poor diet may not be eating folate-rich foods in the first place, or taking a multivitamin with folic acid in it. Add this to the fact that her larger body size may mean her nutrient requirements are increased, says Dr. Gary Kramer, a Miami-based pediatrician. Moreover, being overweight increases the risk of preeclampsia, or high blood pressure during pregnancy. It also increases the risk of gestational diabetes, a condition that can lead to the birth of an overweight child, with associated heart conditions, kidney disease, and other abnormalities.

Boost Fertility

The plan satisfies your pregnancy nutrient requirements, improving your chances of delivering a healthy baby. On the flip side, eating poorly can increase the risk of obesity, which has been associated with birth defects and with PCOS (polycystic ovarian syndrome), a leading cause of infertility. PCOS is characterized by insulin resistance, which can develop as a result of eating foods high in sugar and refined carbohydrates. By consuming fruits, vegetables, whole grains, protein, and "A" and "B" snacks, you are optimizing your likelihood of having a problem-free pregnancy.

Folic Acid–Rich Breakfast Foods for Fertility

The breakfasts on the plan are loaded with folic acid. This B vitamin, also known as folate in foods, is abundant in berries, oranges, spinach, asparagus, beans, whole grain breads, and fortified cereals. Folic acid is critical for the formation of the neural tube, which develops into the baby's spine. Lots of research has concluded that consuming an adequate amount of folic acid can protect against neural-tube defects such as spina bifida, in which there is no fusion of the spinal column, and meningoceal, another malformation of the spinal column and canal (this is the inside portion of the spine, where nerves exist). In fact, it's thought that up to 70 percent of spina bifida cases could be prevented if all women supplemented their diets with 400 micrograms of folic acid around the time of conception and during pregnancy. According to researchers from Texas A&M University, the mechanism underlying the vitamin's protective effect is unknown, but it is likely to include genes that regulate folate transport and metabolism.

By eating a breakfast rich in folic acid, you will improve your prospects of enjoying a healthy pregnancy. Additionally, I recommend taking a supplement or fortified food with 400 micrograms of folic acid every day, for insurance. Even if you are not currently pregnant, as long as you are of childbearing age and planning on having children, make it a point to get your 400 mcg daily. The vitamin is critical to fetal development during the first trimester of pregnancy, and often women don't find out that they are pregnant until weeks after conception. So, be sure to supplement your diet with folic acid as long as you desire children, to help ensure that you will be in fabulous fertility shape.

While it's strongly advisable to supplement your diet with 400 mcg of folic acid prior to and during pregnancy, much higher doses may cause harm. Taking more than 1,000 micrograms of folic acid daily can increase the risk of neurological damage to the fetus. (The upper limit does not apply to folate from food sources.)

Calcium and Iron: Important Fertility Nutrients

Make sure you're consuming foods rich in calcium and iron before you become pregnant. Calcium is needed for build-

Folate Content of Foods

FOOD	SERVING SIZE	MCG OF FOLATE	% DAILY VALUE (BASED ON 400 MCG)
Chicken liver	3.5 ounces	770	193
Breakfast cereals	½ to 1½ cups	100 to 400	25 to 100
Lentils, cooked	½ cup	180	45
Chickpeas	½ cup	141	35
Asparagus	½ cup	132	33
Spinach, cooked	½ cup	131	33
Black beans	½ cup	128	32
Burritos with beans	2	118	30
Pasta	2 ounces	100 to 120	25 to 30
Kidney beans	½ cup	115	29
Cereal bars	1 bar	40 to 100	10 to 25
Lima beans	½ cup	78	20
Tomato juice	1 cup	48	12
Brussels sprouts	½ cup	47	12
Oranges	1 medium	47	12
Broccoli, cooked	½ cup	39	10
Wheat germ	2 tablespoons	38	10

Sources: Food Values of Portions Commonly Used, *16th edition;* FDA Consumer

ing bones and teeth, and if you don't consume enough, your fetus will take calcium from your stores, putting you at risk for bone loss, and possibly osteoporosis later on in life.

Iron is necessary for the formation of hemoglobin, a protein in red blood cells that helps to transport oxygen to the body's cells. During pregnancy, extra iron is needed so that your blood can carry an adequate supply of oxygen to the fetus's cells. (Your blood volume, including red blood cells, will double to deliver additional nutrients for fetal development.) If your diet is rich in iron before pregnancy, your body will store some, which the fetus can use to make hemoglobin during growth.

If you've been adhering to the plan and not skipping your "B" snacks, your calcium intake is adequate. Likewise, if you consume dried fruit for "A" snacks, and fortified cereals such as Total and whole-grain breads, you will build up your iron stores. A multivitamin will also help you to meet your iron needs. For the protein portion of your meals, I recommend incorporating scallops, oysters, clams, or mussels, which are rich in iron. If you have a history of anemia, you should talk to your doctor about taking an iron supplement (in addition to a multivitamin/multimineral) prior to getting pregnant.

Watch Vitamin A

While vitamin A is necessary for fetal growth, too much can increase the risk of birth defects during pregnancy. A recent study in the *New England Journal of Medicine* found that 1 in 57 babies whose mothers consumed high levels of vitamin A—more than 10,000 international units (IU) of preformed vitamin A from supplements—had a malformation attributable to high doses of the vitamin. (Preformed vitamin A is different from beta-carotene, the nontoxic form of vitamin A that exists in foods including carrots, sweet potatoes, and cantaloupe.) If you're taking supplements, check to make sure they don't contain more than 3,000 IU of vitamin A, to play it safe. In addition to supplements, liver contains high levels of preformed vitamin A. (You won't find liver on your plan; however, if you do eat liver regularly, be sure to limit it now!) Accutane and Retin-A (drugs used to treat acne) are naturally occurring derivatives of vitamin A and should be avoided as well.

Fertility Fact Check: Avoid These Behaviors

Because alcohol can increase the risk of miscarriage and birth defects, it should be avoided as long as you are trying to conceive. Alcohol also increases the risk of fetal alcohol syndrome, which can result in facial abnormalities, growth retardation, and dysfunction of the central nervous system. As little as one to two drinks per day can cause a miscarriage or can result in a low-birth-weight baby. Use of marijuana and other drugs can result in similar problems and should be stopped at least one month before you plan to conceive. Tobacco use should be avoided as well, as smoking has been linked to infant death, low-birth-weight babies, preterm deliveries, and respiratory illnesses, including asthma.

It's wise to cut back on your caffeine consumption while trying to conceive. Up to 300 milligrams (mg) per day appears to be safe (that's about three cups of coffee); more than this amount can result in fertility problems.

Healthy Pregnancy

During pregnancy, your nutrient needs increase to support the growth of a fetus. The first step is to choose a meal plan and calorie level that you can follow for weight maintenance—in other words, a calorie level at which you are not gaining or losing weight. Then, you can simply add a bowl of cereal with a serving of fruit and skim milk—to get your extra pregnancy nutrition in. Remember, during pregnancy, the goal is weight *gain*, not loss.

Weight Gain During Pregnancy

Once you are pregnant, it's time to put aside any weight-loss goals you previously had and focus on just the opposite: increasing your poundage. Watching the number on the scale increase during pregnancy is a positive thing, as weight gain during this time will help to ensure delivery of a healthy baby. Not gaining enough during pregnancy increases the possibility of delivering a low-birth-weight baby, who may suffer from respiratory and other problems.

The actual amount of weight you should gain during pregnancy depends on your weight at the time you conceive. If you are at a healthy body weight (a BMI of 19.8 to 26—say, a 5'4" woman weighing 120 pounds), your weight-gain goal should be 25 to 35 pounds. If you are overweight (a BMI of between 26 and 29—or, a woman at the same height weighing 155 pounds), your goal is less: 15 to 25 pounds. And if you are underweight (a BMI of less than 19.8, or a woman 5′4″ who weighs 110 pounds), your goal is 28 to 40 pounds. This is assuming you are not having twins; if you are, your goal is 35 to 45 pounds.

In the first trimester, your weight gain may be only a few pounds—anywhere from two to five. In the second and third trimesters, you should aim to gain approximately a pound per week—slightly more if you are underweight, and slightly less if you're overweight.

Pregnancy Pounds

During pregnancy, your calorie and nutrient needs increase to support the growth of the life inside you. Weight gain during pregnancy is an indication that the fetus has the nutrients needed for growth and development. Here's where the weight gain comes from:

Baby	7.5 pounds
Placenta	1.5 pounds
Fluids and blood volume	7 pounds
Uterus	2 pounds
Fat deposits	7 pounds
Breasts	1 pound
Total	**26 pounds**

Note: These are averages; individual weight gain will vary among women.

Nutritional Needs During Pregnancy

Moms-to-be don't necessarily have to eat for two, but it's important to meet increased demands for calories, protein, calcium, folic acid, and iron. Here's how your nutrient requirements and weight goals change during pregnancy.

- **Calories.** Calorie needs increase to support the energy needs of both mother and fetus. Again, this is not to say you have to "eat for two." *About 300 extra calories each day in the second trimester and approximately 450 in the third trimester is the goal.*
- **Protein.** Protein serves as the building material for the fetus's cells, and so needs are greater during pregnancy. An extra 25 grams of protein per day above nonpregnancy needs is the recommended daily amount. This looks like three decks of

cards in terms of portion sizes of fish or chicken.

- **Calcium.** While calcium requirements are the same for pregnant and nonpregnant 30-something women (1,000 mg per day), you can't afford to fall short at this time. Remember, if you don't get enough calcium, your baby will take what it needs from your bones, putting you at risk for osteoporosis later on. I would also take a calcium supplement containing 500 mg of calcium at this time (see more on calcium supplements in Chapter 4).

- **Folic acid.** Your need for folic acid increases during pregnancy to 600 micrograms each day. In addition to providing protection against birth defects, the vitamin directly assists in the development of new body cells during pregnancy.

- **Iron.** Iron needs increase by about a third during pregnancy, from 18 mg per day to 27 mg. Iron is needed for making hemoglobin, a protein in red blood cells that carries oxygen to the body's cells and to the fetus. All pregnant women should

Eating for Pregnancy

Instead of worrying about counting calories during pregnancy, you can simply have any of the following options in addition to a balanced, nutrient-dense diet for weight maintenance (note: portions can be slightly larger during the third trimester):

- A bowl of Total cereal with a half cup of skim milk and a small banana
- A light multigrain English muffin (fortified with calcium, iron, and folic acid) with two table-spoons of peanut butter
- Half of a chicken breast sandwich and a serving of calcium-fortified pudding

In addition to helping you hit your calorie target, these minimeals will supplement your protein, iron, calcium, and folic acid intake—all critical nutrients for fetal growth.

take a supplement containing iron, to ensure adequate intake
and to lessen the risk of becoming anemic during pregnancy.

● **Prenatal vitamins.** I recommend taking a prenatal vitamin
containing iron, calcium, and folic acid, in light of the
increased nutrient requirements during pregnancy. (The
increased iron need during pregnancy can be particularly
difficult to meet from foods alone.) A prenatal vitamin is all
the more important if you are vegan, if you're having more
than one baby, or if you simply have poor eating habits.

Moms-to-Be: Get Your Omega-3s Without the Mercury

We already covered the health benefits of omega-3 fats in
fish, including their role in lowering heart disease risk and
promoting skin health. Beyond those attributes, one type
of omega-3 fat, known as docoasahexaenoic acid (DHA), is
essential for fetal brain and eye development. But many
moms-to-be have a new concern: mercury in fish.

Mercury can affect the nervous system of a growing fetus.
Fish absorb a form of mercury known as methylmercury,
putting you at risk when you consume fish with high levels.
All of this is not to say you should avoid fish—but it's time to
switch to species that are lower in mercury.

The most recent FDA advisory recommends that pregnant women, women of childbearing age, nursing mothers,
and young children limit their portions of albacore tuna to
6 ounces per week. (The recommendation was based on a
sampling of more than 3,700 cans of tuna.) In addition to
limiting albacore tuna, women of childbearing age should
avoid shark, swordfish, tilefish, and king mackerel, because
of their high mercury levels. Because ahi tuna steaks (i.e., big
eye) can be high in mercury, I recommend avoiding these as
well.

I am also an advocate of limiting your total fish intake
to three small meals per week (that's about 12 ounces, if

you've been consuming 4-ounce portions). Choose fish and shellfish that are low in mercury, such as shrimp, herring, salmon, sole, tilapia, cod, crab, scallops, flounder, and catfish.

Focus on Fish Oils

As just discussed, DHA is necessary for brain and eye development of a growing fetus (the fatty acid actually exists in the gray matter of the brain and retina of the eye), especially in the third trimester. The fetus relies on the mother to meet those DHA needs, so moms-to-be must meet their needs through omega-3 fats in fish or, if not eating at least two fish meals per week, other sources of omega-3s such as walnuts, flaxseeds, and omega-3 fortified eggs.

Sources of Safe Omega-3 Fats

Catfish
Cod
Crab
Flounder
Herring
Oysters
Salmon
Sardines
Scallops
Shrimp
Sole
Tilapia
Trout (freshwater)
Whitefish

Source: Based on Mercury Levels in Commercial Fish and Shellfish *(Food and Drug Administration)*

Recent research tells us that DHA may also provide moms with protection against postpartum depression, which affects about 10 percent of women. One recent study found that a 1 percent increase in blood DHA was associated with a 59 percent reduction in depressive symptoms among women with postpartum depression.

If a mother's intake of DHA is low, the fetus will take what it needs, putting the mother at increased risk. So, it's important for moms-to-be to consume fish oils, but avoid fish that contain high levels of mercury. See the accompanying sidebar, "Sources of Safe Omega-3 Fats."

Other Nutritional Concerns During Pregnancy

Here are some additional nutritional concerns during pregnancy, along with my recommendations.

Caffeinated Beverages

If you are a heavy consumer of caffeinated beverages, I urge you to restrain your consumption while you're pregnant. In general, pregnant women should limit their daily intake to no more than one cup of coffee or other caffeinated beverage, including soda, caffeinated tea, and energy drinks. If you don't typically drink caffeinated beverages, now is not the time to take up the habit.

One reason for avoidance is that consuming high amounts of caffeine may increase the risks of miscarriage and of having a low-birth-weight baby. A recent study found that drinking five cups of coffee each day more than doubles a woman's risk of miscarriage. Caffeine can also cause a slight calcium loss in the urine, and in light of the importance of calcium, especially during pregnancy, that's something that moms-to-be don't need. Another thing they don't need is heartburn, which can be exacerbated by caffeine.

Artificial Sweeteners

While at most other times I'm fine with the idea of consuming a modest amount of foods that contain artificial or non-

Sushi Sacrifice

Cooking fish does not affect its mercury level, which means that raw versus cooked is not a factor in that regard. Still, when you're pregnant, you should not eat sushi, regardless of the mercury concern, because pregnancy puts you at higher risk for acquiring illness from raw foods. There is too much potential for contamination, so it's best to err on the side of safety: sacrifice the sushi if you're expecting.

nutritive sweeteners to help you achieve your weight-loss goals, artificial sweeteners should be severely restricted, if not eliminated, during pregnancy. First of all, saccharin can cross the placenta, and there is controversy as to whether it is safe. Additionally, women with phenylketonuria, a genetic condition also called simply PKU, should avoid aspartame-containing foods and beverages at all times. Notwithstanding these caveats, the main reason to forgo nonnutritive sweeteners during pregnancy is that they enable you to reduce calorie intake, which is contraindicated during pregnancy. They may also crowd out more nutritious foods and beverages. For example, if you're drinking diet sodas instead of milk, your calcium intake may be less than optimal.

Listeria-Containing Foods

Pregnant women are 20 times more likely than healthy adults to get listeriosis—a foodborne infection that can result in miscarriage as well as fetal death. For this reason, foods that may contain listeria should be avoided. These include soft cheeses, such as Brie, goat, and feta, as well as Camembert, Roquefort, and queso blanco fresco (Mexican-style cheese). Sushi, other raw or undercooked foods, hot dogs, and lunchmeat should also be excluded.

Shedding Postpregnancy Pounds

Postpartum is a complicated time for most women. You're a new mom, which is exciting and delightful. But you also, somehow, gained a new body along the way. The radical changes to your body may leave you wondering: What happened to my figure?

Take heart: by continuing to trust the plan as your guide, you will be able to shed "baby fat" after you've recovered from giving birth! Your calorie needs will differ, however, depending on whether you are breast-feeding. If you're not breast-feeding, you can resume a calorie-controlled diet—specifically, one that calls for about 300 fewer calories than what you were consuming during pregnancy. If you are breast-feeding, your calorie needs remain higher—about 300 to 400 calories above your maintenance needs, or the amount that allowed you to maintain your weight before you became pregnant.

Keep in mind, a minimum of 1,800 calories daily is usually needed to provide sufficient energy and nutrients for breast-feeding. If you're not sure how many calories you need, you can start by adding a 200-calorie snack to the 1,600-calorie meal plan (you can simply add an extra "A" and "B" snack). Rest assured: in the beginning weeks, your hunger level will probably guide you as to when and how much you should eat.

Breast-Feeding Burns Calories

Breast-feeding is a calorie-burning activity, and it can allow you to lose anywhere from one-half pound to one pound per week. The extra calories you consume are used to produce milk and are not going toward your waist. Additionally, some of your fat reserves from pregnancy—about 200 calories' worth—are mobilized and used toward milk production.

Also note that after you give birth, a "postpartum diuresis" will occur. This is simply a fluid loss, related to fluid weight gain during pregnancy (about 30 percent of the weight gained during pregnancy is fluids). This loss of fluid will result in your dropping pounds quickly, and there's no need to eat more to compensate for this.

In addition to breast-feeding, exercising will help postpartum women lose weight. Moms can usually start about six weeks after delivery, with a doctor's approval. While aerobic exercise doesn't seem to have an adverse affect on milk production, I don't recommend strenuous exercise during breast-feeding.

As you can see, there's no call for concern about shedding postpregnancy pounds. The weight will come off, at a safe, slow rate. Keep in mind that losing more than five pounds per month can interfere with the quality of breast milk.

Nutritional Needs During Breast-Feeding

After your baby is born, you can continue to take your prenatal vitamins while breast-feeding. Along with extra calories, your diet should yield some important nutrients for optimal milk production, and if it comes up short in these nutrients, your milk may be low in them as well.

Your protein needs increase by 25 grams when breast-feeding (that's equivalent to about three and a half ounces of chicken or fish). Your B vitamins, including B_{12}, B_6, and folic acid, are equally important, and if you don't get enough, your milk will supply less of them.

Continue supplementing your diet with iron, especially if you are anemic, as anemia may result in the production of less milk. Calcium continues to perform a primary role during breast-feeding as well, and 1,000 mg is the amount to aim for (the same amount during and before pregnancy). Vitamin D remains important as well. While your zinc needs also increase during breast-feeding, a multi or prenatal should suffice.

To meet your fluid needs, aim for 12 eight-ounce cups of low-fat milk, water, or juice each day. It's best to continue to limit coffee, tea, and other caffeine-containing beverages, and to avoid alcohol.

Emily's Story

When I first met Emily, she filled me in on the need-to-know details of her weight history. "During my pregnancy, I gained 55 pounds on top of the extra 20 to 30 I was carrying before I got pregnant." Eager to shed the extra weight, Emily figured no time could be better for trying a new approach to dieting, and she set herself a goal of losing close to 30 pounds. She had a specific area in mind from which she wanted to see the weight disappear—"the spare tire" around her abdomen, left over from a C-section.

Dieting is no new venture for Emily. Since the age of 13, she's been on and off of a long list of diets, headed by Weight Watchers. Though she had some success with some diets, nothing lasted. But she thinks she knows why. A former marathon runner, being active was not Emily's downfall. It was portion control. "I don't eat junk. I don't veg out in front of the TV with a bag of chips and a pint of ice cream. But I do love to eat good food, and more often than not, I will clean my plate even when full." Emily says she gets a lot of pleasure from food, partly because she has training as a chef.

Emily soon discovered that dieting is a different world when you're trying it postpartum. Her already crowded schedule was now even more hectic with a newborn needing constant attention. What mattered most to Emily was to have a diet that would provide sufficient calories and nutrients for a breast-feeding mommy.

Emily had been consuming 1,600 calories, so one of the first adjustments I made was increasing her calories to 1,800 a day. This would provide her with enough energy for breast-feeding without sabotaging her weight-loss efforts. To attain the increased-caloric goal, I instructed her to follow the 1,600 calorie plan, and told her to double up on "A" and "B" snacks. While most of us would be thrilled to double our snacking, Emily wasn't so psyched. For a harried new mom, more snacking immediately translates to more planning, preparing, and cleaning. Fortunately, like many other women, Emily proved to be a pro at devising a multitasking solution. She solved her snacking snafu with the power of the smoothie. She tries to have a smoothie a day made of milk, frozen berries, and half a banana—which incorporates "A" and "B" snacks at the same time! After a few days of accelerated snacking, Emily found that eating every few hours coordinated well with her breast-feeding schedule.

Emily found that her meal and snack options on The 30s Health Prescription were quick and easy with staples such as cereal with fruit, English muffins with Swiss cheese and tomato, and turkey sandwiches. It was carving out time for preparing veggie-ful dinners that was a bit of a challenge for Emily, who considered veggies a pain to prepare. Though she loves to cook, this new mom is busy, busy, busy. She wasn't about to fuss over having a steady supply of fresh produce at hand and then concocting a palette-pleasing way of preparing it. Her husband (who became an honorary participant in the plan) helped her overcome this produce problem. They found their solution in the form of packaged greens or romaine hearts that would make for a quick dinner salad; bags of frozen veggies also became a staple.

With time and practice, Emily has become more familiar with the portions and has been able to be more flexible with the meals (i.e., designing her own). She says that breakfasts and lunches are the easiest, because they most closely resemble what she was eating prior to the diet—just with smaller portions. One sacrifice Emily and her husband had to make was their habit of ordering in, because the take-in food they like has a lot more fat than is allowed on the diet, and the portions are usually too big.

After just four weeks, Emily's sacrifices paid off. She lost nine pounds and noticed that the "tire" around her midsection was deflating! Emily also reports that people have told her that her skin looks great and adds that her energy level is surprisingly good, considering the interrupted sleep from breast-feeding throughout the night.

One of the best aspects of the plan for Emily is that she could follow it without constant hunger reminding her that she was on a diet. "The snacks help me feel satisfied," she says. "Other diets give you a food allowance that you can eat at one sitting if you wish; this plan tells you to distribute your meals and snacks throughout the day, and that keeps you feeling 'full' throughout the day as well." She especially looks forward to her daily "C" snack, noting: "I don't feel deprived at all because on this diet I can have a daily 'treat.' I also don't obsess about being on a diet."

To date, Emily has lost 48 pounds on the plan!

Enjoying Nights Out

(10)

ow it's time to address how to stick to an eating plan while you're enjoying life and all the culinary enticements it serves up. Well, I'm here to tell you that you *can* be loyal to the principles of the plan during business dinners, social events, parties, and other fun nights out. It does take a little bit of planning, however, as Robin learned.

✳ Robin's Story

Robin's lifestyle is not exactly "diet friendly." As a recently married publishing professional, she said that, for her, food was something she typically encountered between meetings during long, exhausting days at the office. And she's not talking about health food. Robin would get so ravenously hungry that she would turn to the chips, cookies, or whatever else was commonly available in the workplace to satiate her appetite. Plus, as is the story with many other New Yorkers, Robin lived with another impediment to eating well: a kitchen way too small for comfort. Then, enter her husband, and the obstacles to maintaining a healthy weight just started piling up. "The second I met my husband, I started to put on weight," she says.

Typical of many couples, the newlyweds centered much of their social lives on food. Calendar activities would encompass dining out with friends, meeting for drinks during weeknights, and attending family events involving "child-friendly" fare such as pizza and ice cream. Robin's food-frenzy lifestyle became a problem. "When I socialize, I lose control over what I eat and what I order," she admitted.

As a consequence, dieting became a fixture in Robin's life. Atkins came first. Then Jenny Craig. She took a stab at Weight Watchers when she got engaged, and again after the wedding. Nothing had staying power. Whereas she'd never really had to "work" to keep in shape before her mid-20s, now her body was being less cooperative. "Once I hit my 30s, my body completely changed," she states.

Robin and I first reviewed some of her goals. She wanted to take off enough weight to permanently retire her "fat clothes," get and stay healthy, and prepare her body for pregnancy. Robin's father had a heart attack at the age of 34 and recently underwent a triple bypass. She also has a family history of high cholesterol.

I explained the concept of making a third of her plate protein, a third vegetables, and a third grains at each meal. "A" snacks were unappealing to Robin, but she gave high marks to the combo of dried cranberries and peanuts.

Because her job and her social life were solid obstacles, Robin's success would depend on good planning. She would have to allot time each week to plan out her meals so she could avoid such pitfalls as bingeing after all-day meetings and overindulging at a friend's birthday dinner.

Robin's strategies included taking yogurt and fruit to her work meetings. This allowed her to get her "A" and "B" snacks in during the day without sabotaging her weight-loss efforts by grabbing cookies and candy. At restaurants, she sticks with her plan by ordering two appetizers—maybe a shrimp cocktail and a salad—instead of a main course. She also frequently logs on to her computer before heading out to a restaurant and peruses the menu in advance, so she can get a jump start on what to order. For family gatherings, Robin fills up ahead of time on her snacks so she doesn't succumb to the attraction of hamburgers and desserts. She learned that by adopting this routine, she was less inclined to cheat and waste her efforts.

Thanks to her commitment, Robin lost nine pounds by week 10 of the plan. "The plan has fit in nicely to my lifestyle. It has made me a better eater, and mentally, that makes me feel better because I know I am making better decisions for my health."

Robin emphasizes that she was able to stick with it not only because she is meticulous about planning meals but also because whenever she's at a restaurant, party, business meeting, or other event, she *thinks* about what she's eating and savors every bite. And, she points out, the plan is simple enough for anyone to master: "Picturing your plate in thirds is so easy. If I can stick with it, anyone can."

Stay Slim and Healthy When Dining Out and About

Eating healthfully when dining out and socializing is probably one of the most imposing challenges for 30-something women. With so many tantalizing food choices and, at the same time, so many culinary unknowns—such as how the food is prepared, or even the ingredients used—it can be tough going. And, of course, that doesn't take into account the lure of drinks and dessert. It's not impossible to stay slim and healthy when you are dining out and enjoying social events, but as with your weekly meals, you need to think it through ahead of time.

Salad Strategy

You can enjoy a restaurant meal without doing damage to your diet and waistline. In fact, research from Penn State University suggests you can dine out and still lose weight, especially if you order a low-calorie salad as an appetizer.

In the study, a group of women were required to eat an entire low-calorie salad before eating a pasta meal of cheese tortellini with tomato sauce (they could eat as much pasta as they liked). The salad comprised iceberg and romaine lettuce, carrots, tomatoes, celery, cucumbers, fat-free dressing, and light mozzarella cheese.

When women ate one and a half cups of the salad (which provided 50 calories), they ate 7 percent (64) fewer calories for the whole meal compared to when they skipped the salad. When they ate three cups of salad before having their pasta (for a total of 100 calories), they ate even less for the entire meal (12 percent, or 107 fewer calories), compared with their consumption when they skipped the salad.

I love this study, because it illustrates how you can dine out, order an appetizer, and still limit your overall calorie intake! While adding an appetizer usually increases the total amount of calories consumed at a meal, this study shows that when the first course is a large portion of a low-calorie salad, with lots of fiber-rich vegetables, you feel less hungry when the meal arrives and eat fewer calories for the entire meal.

Keep in mind here that only a low-calorie salad will do the trick. When women ate a small, high-calorie salad (200 calories) with more cheese and higher-fat dressing, they ate *more* at the meal (8 percent, or 71 more calories overall) than they ate when not having salad at all. And when they ate a large, high-calorie salad, they ate 17 percent, or 145 calories, more at the meal, versus no salad. So, clearly, the type of salad is the determinant, and according to this study, it must be low in calories.

Salads: Calorie Culprits Versus Slimming Substitutes

CALORIE CULPRIT			SLIMMING SUBSTITUTE
Four black, super colossal olives	=	50 calories	=	Sixteen cherry tomatoes
One ounce of shredded cheddar cheese	=	115 calories	=	Two and a half ounces of low-fat goat cheese
One half cup of croutons made with oil	=	145 calories	=	Twelve fat-free saltines
One quarter of a cup of dried cranberries	=	95 calories	=	One cup of mandarin orange sections
One tablespoon of full-fat ranch dressing	=	75 calories	=	One and a half table-spoons of reduced-fat ranch dressing
One tablespoon of chunky blue cheese dressing	=	65 calories	=	Three tablespoons of creamy low-fat blue cheese dressing

Source: ESHA database

Low-calorie salads don't have to be unappealing. According to Barbara Rolls, Ph.D., lead author of the study, the subjects were not very sensitive to changes in the fat content of the salads (they guessed the same fat content for both low- and higher-calorie salads, even though fat ranged from 14 to 65 percent), and the lower-calorie, lower-fat salads were well liked.

When eating salads, choosing low-fat or fat-free dressings is the ideal approach. If you opt for high-fat varieties, have your dressing on the side and use no more than one tablespoon.

Two-Appetizer Strategy

The portions you receive at restaurants are usually huge, and you don't always know how the food is prepared. In these situations, my number one strategy is to order two appetizers: a low-calorie salad (or vegetable) and a protein-rich dish. As you now know, eating a low-calorie salad is beneficial for weight loss, as it can help you to consume fewer calories for the entire meal. In addition, having a protein-rich appetizer instead of an entree will help you keep your portions as close to your plan as possible. If you prefer soup to salad, you can go that route as long as you order one that is broth based (not made with cream).

Examples of appetizer combos are tuna tartar with a salad; grilled chicken skewers with edamame or seaweed salad; and shrimp cocktail with grilled vegetables. If you are not keen on the appetizer selections, or you're swayed by other menu offerings, you can share an entree and order a side salad. By heeding this advice, you will succeed at keeping your calories in check when you have limited control over what's set before you.

Dining Tips

Staying on your plan when dining out is all about strategy. Again, ordering two appetizers—one low-calorie salad or broth-based soup and one

Portion Distortion!

A study from Penn State delivers some less exciting news: we eat more when we're served larger portions at restaurants, and we can't tell large from small! In the experiment, the size of a baked ziti course served in a restaurant varied between a standard portion and a larger serving containing 50 percent more food. When customers were served the larger portion of ziti, they ate nearly all of it, adding on an extra 172 calories to the meal. Despite the extra calories consumed, the diners rated the size of both portions as equally appropriate!

In a similar study, involving submarine sandwiches, in the *Journal of the American Dietetic Association*, individuals were offered sandwiches 6, 8, 10, and 12 inches long for lunch on different days. Women ate an extra 159 calories, or 31 percent more, when served the largest sandwich, compared with the smallest.

If you have trouble eyeballing portion sizes on your plan when dining out, see Appendix C, "Visualizing Portions on the Plan."

protein dish—is your smartest move. Still, it can be challenging to navigate the dining scene, so I'm going to share with
you my top five tips for smooth passage when you're eating at
restaurants.

1. **Pick the restaurant.** By selecting your dining destination,
   you're putting yourself in control of your food options and
   making it easier to stick to your plan. I tell my female friends
   and clients to have two favorite restaurants to suggest at all
   times when deciding on where to eat.
2. **Get menus faxed ahead of time.** Perusing the menu before
   you dine gives you additional time to review your options—
   especially important if you don't know the restaurant. Some
   restaurants also publish their menus online.
3. **Know the code words for fat and calories.** Don't fall into
   hidden fat traps when ordering from menus. See the sidebar
   entitled "Menu Terms That Imply Higher Fat."
4. **Choose dishes that are prepared with minimal fat.** Know the
   preparation methods that are associated with low-fat, low-
   calorie foods. See the companion sidebar, "Menu Terms That
   Imply Lower Fat."
5. **If necessary, special-order your food.** If you don't like what
   you see on the menu, ask if your dietary preferences can be
   accommodated. You may want to call ahead to find this out.

Restaurant Recommendations

Following are some healthful options to consider when dining
out on different cuisines. All of these incorporate antiaging
plates of protein, vegetables, and grains. In some cases, you
may wish to add a side of vegetables, a bit more protein, or a
grain to round out your plate, so it fits the prescription of one-
third protein, one-third vegetables, and one-third grains.

Japanese Cuisine

My friends and I are wild about Japanese, and lucky us, because Japanese foods such as sushi, sashimi, and teriyaki fish dishes are all perfectly suited for The 30s Health Prescription. The biggest challenge to eating Japanese is decoding the menu, with unfamiliar words such as *oshinko* (Japanese pickled vegetables) and *donburi* (rice in a bowl, topped with chicken or meat). High-calorie loads in Japanese food come from deep-fried tempura dishes and from sushi rolls that have spicy, creamy sauce, cream cheese, or lots of avocado.

RECOMMENDATIONS FOR JAPANESE CUISINE

- Broiled (yakimono) shrimp, salmon, or any other seafood or shellfish, and miso soup
- Tuna, yellowtail, and salmon sashimi, and oshitashi (boiled spinach with fish stock) or a side salad
- Lobster maki with mango; shrimp and asparagus maki
- Salmon teriyaki, steamed vegetables, and brown rice
- Broiled scallops and a side of edamame or seaweed salad
- Yosenabe (chicken, seafood, and vegetables in broth) and a side salad

Menu Terms That Imply Lower Fat

Cooking Terms
Au jus (with broth)
Baked (cooked with dry heat in an oven)
Braised (simmered in a small amount of liquid over low heat)
Broiled (cooked directly under a heat source)
En papillote (steamed in a paper bag or parchment paper)
Grilled (cooked directly over a heat source)
Poached (cooked in liquid, below boiling)
Roasted (cooked uncovered with dry heat)
Steamed (cooked with steam rising from boiling water)

Sauces
Reduction (broth or pan juices)
Vinaigrette (oil and vinegar)
Marinara (tomato, onion, garlic, basil)
Dijonaise (Dijon mustard, white wine)

Note: Limit protein to four ounces and rice to half-cup portions.

STEER CLEAR OF THESE

- Spider Leg (fried soft-shell crab)
- Tempura dishes (deep-fried)
- Agemono dishes (dipped in bread crumbs and deep-fried)
- Philadelphia roll (lox and cream cheese)

Note: Green tea, a popular Japanese beverage, is rich in antioxidants and may offer metabolism benefits (see Chapter 2).

Italian Cuisine

Italian cuisine offers lots of healthful choices. Two of its hallmarks are antiaging ingredients: olive oil, which is rich in monounsaturated fats, those that can lower LDL (low-density lipoprotein)—the harmful cholesterol; and tomato sauce, which is rich in lycopene, an ingredient that may help guard women

Menu Terms That Imply Higher Fat

Cooking Terms

Au gratin (with cheese)
Creamy (using cream or eggs)
Crispy (fried)
En croute (in a crust)
Sautéed (cooked quickly in small amount of fat)
Stir-fried (cooked quickly in oil over high heat)
Scalloped (with cream)

Sauces

Alfredo (butter, heavy cream, Parmesan cheese)
Béarnaise (white wine, vinegar, tarragon, shallots, egg yolk, butter)
Béchamel (milk, flour, butter, onion)
Beurre blanc (wine, vinegar, shallot reduction, cold butter)
Bolognese (ground beef, pork, ham, butter/olive oil)
Carbonara (cream, egg, Parmesan cheese, bacon)
Hollandaise (egg yolk, butter, lemon juice)

against cardiovascular disease and cancer, through its antioxidant effects. Additionally, with primavera and antipasto dishes you get vegetables, whose vitamins and phytochemicals may protect against disease. If you can't resist ordering

pasta, request a half portion, and make sure it includes protein and vegetables.

RECOMMENDATIONS FOR ITALIAN CUISINE

- Mussels, a slice of bread, and a mesclun salad with balsamic vinaigrette dressing
- Minestrone soup (vegetarian), tuna carpaccio/tartar, and a roll
- Shrimp cocktail and grilled vegetable antipasto
- Linguine with clams (half portion) and a mixed green salad
- Angel hair pasta with shrimp (half portion) and marinara sauce (or a little bit of olive oil), and a side of steamed spinach
- Broiled salmon, broccoli rabe (in light oil), and cannellini beans with a side salad

Note: If the restaurant doesn't serve half portions, you can share with a friend, or you can eat half and take the rest home.

STEER CLEAR OF THESE

- Mozzarella in carozza (fried cheese—in a "carriage")
- Parmigiana dishes (deep-fried and covered with cheese)
- Alfredo, vodka, bolognese, and carbonara sauces
- Creamy dressings such as creamy Italian or creamy Caesar
- Manicotti and lasagna (often loaded with high-fat cheese)
- Buttery garlic bread and focaccia
- Risotto made with a lot of butter

Note: Marsala sauce is made from marsala wine and chicken or vegetable stock, but it can have oil, butter, or cream in it. Be sure to ask how it's prepared.

Chinese Cuisine

Chinese food can be a diet delight or a disaster, depending on how you order. Many of the fats in Chinese food are hid-den, which can make it tricky. For example, meats may be fried but then coated with sauce, so you can't always tell. Also, Chinese sauces can be high in sugar. Plum sauce, for example, is made with plum jam and brown sugar, and sweet-and-sour sauce usually contains sugar as well as cornstarch (a source of sugar), to thicken it.

The positive aspect is that Chinese dishes present lots of fish options and vegetables, which makes it easy to create a 30s plate, especially with fiber-rich brown rice. Also, green tea, a popular Chinese (and Japanese) beverage, may offer metabolism-boosting benefits, as mentioned in Chapter 2.

RECOMMENDATIONS FOR CHINESE CUISINE

- Hot-and-sour soup, steamed scallops, and mixed vegetables
- Steamed shrimp with mixed vegetables and brown rice
- Steamed chicken with broccoli and brown rice
- Tofu in black bean sauce and steamed string beans

Note: Because Chinese restaurants often serve large portions, I recommend sharing all dishes. Limit protein to four ounces and rice to half-cup portions.

Olive Oil Versus Butter

In research from the University of Illinois, hidden cameras showed that diners who put olive oil, rather than butter, on their bread ate more fat and calories per piece—but in the end, they ate less bread.

A total of 341 customers were randomly given either olive oil or butter to accompany their bread at an Italian restaurant. Following their dinner, the amount of bread eaten by each diner was calculated. The researchers found that use of olive oil outpaced use of butter by 26 percent; per slice, that translated to 40 calories versus 33 calories. But, the olive oil users ate 23 percent *less* bread during the meal compared with their buttering friends. In other words, olive oil users had a heavier hand when it came to dipping, but they consumed fewer calories from their bread overall: an average of 264 versus 319.

While olive oil is healthful for the heart, it will contribute 9 calories per gram, or about 120 calories per tablespoon. The moral: Choose olive oil over butter when having your bread. Just don't dip for too long!

STEER CLEAR OF THESE

- Fried noodles and fried rice
- Fried egg rolls, fried spring rolls, and fried wontons
- Beef and pork dishes, including spareribs
- Peking duck with skin
- Fried chicken dishes such as sweet-and-sour chicken and General Tsao's chicken

Note: If you like the taste of General Tsao's chicken but don't want the fried coating, ask if you can have it coated lightly with sauce and not fried. Eggdrop soup contains eggs, and possibly oil, while wonton soup contains wonton wrappers, pork, and sesame oil.

Mexican Cuisine

Here's an interesting morsel for lovers of Mexican food: Burritos, chimichangas, and tacos with hard shells—all common in Mexican fast-food restaurants—are not considered authentic Mexican cuisine. In fact, true south-of-the-border cuisine, with its high-fiber meals, can fit nicely into The 30s Health Prescription. Mexican cooking features lots of spices, which can please the palate while sparing extra calories.

RECOMMENDATIONS FOR MEXICAN CUISINE

- Black bean soup or gazpacho and a salad
- Grilled chicken or shrimp fajitas with onion, salsa, and a bit of guacamole
- Two soft corn tortillas with chicken, lettuce, and tomato
- Baked tortilla chips (15) with salsa (or pico de gallo) and ceviche (raw fish soaked in lemon or lime juice)

STEER CLEAR OF THESE

- Quesadillas
- Carnitas (pork cooked in lard)
- Chimichangas (deep-fried flour tortillas filled with beef or chicken and beans)

- Refried beans cooked with lard
- Sour cream, extra cheese, crispy (fried) tortillas, and chorizo (Mexican sausage)

Note: Mexican meals, including fajitas, often come with cheese, guacamole, and sour cream. To keep your calories in check, limit yourself to two tortillas and choose only one "fat" topping. Salsa is always a better accompaniment! Also, beans are rich in soluble fiber, which helps to lower cholesterol levels; however, the lard in which some beans are cooked cancels out the effect. If you have beans, be sure they are cooked without lard.

French Cuisine

French food can be very caloric, so there's no such thing as a free French lunch. For natives, the calorie load is offset by the fact that portions of French food are typically not as large as the type we are served here in the United States. The range of French restaurants here is wide, however, with French bistros typically serving more healthful fare than fancy French restaurants (think grilled fish and vegetables versus nouvelle French cuisine, which incorporates sauces with butter, egg yolk, and cream).

RECOMMENDATIONS FOR FRENCH CUISINE
- Truite au bleu (trout poached in white wine and fish stock)
- Bouillabaisse (fish stew)
- Salade niçoise (salad with tuna, green beans, potatoes, olives, and egg) with dressing on the side
- Steamed mussels, watercress and endive salad, and consommé
- Coq au vin (chicken cooked in red wine)—ask to have the skin removed
- Pot-au-feu of chicken (chicken poached in water and white wine with vegetables)
- Grilled fish and grilled vegetables

Note: Limit fish and chicken portions to four ounces. You can add a half cup of rice or half of a medium-size baked potato (with the skin) to your meal. You can also add a side salad if your meal does not come with vegetables.

STEER CLEAR OF THESE

- Duck confit (*confit* means cooked in its own fat)
- Coquilles St.-Jacques (scallops made with butter and cheese)
- Foie gras (goose liver)
- Dishes made with hollandaise (has egg yolk and butter), béarnaise (same as hollandaise but with tarragon), béchamel (made with whole milk and flour), Mornay (béchamel with cheese), and beurre blanc sauces (mostly butter)

Note: Vegetable-based sauces such as red pepper coulis (pureed) can be healthful, but if they look oily, it may not be worth the calories. Choose dishes with the words *en papillote* (steamed in a paper bag/parchment paper) and *au jus* (with broth).

Thai Cuisine

Similar to Chinese food, Thai contains many vegetables and noodles, but with added spice! Spices include lemongrass, ginger, and cilantro, to name a few. Most American Thai restaurants go mild on taste, however—straying a bit from authentic Thai overseas. Thai food can fit into your 30s plan if you choose wisely and watch portions. The large variety of spices in Thai cuisine will give you lots of flavor without adding extra calories. Be careful with oil-based dishes though, such as pad pak (vegetables sautéed in oil) and pad Thai—a popular dish consisting of stir-fried noodles with bean sprouts, egg, peanuts, and shrimp or chicken.

RECOMMENDATIONS FOR THAI CUISINE

- Gai satay (grilled chicken satay with peanut sauce and cucumber relish) and Thai salad rolls
- Pla bai tong (grilled red snapper in banana leaves with Thai herbs)

- Thai lettuce wraps with chicken or shrimp
- Yum woon sen (cellophane noodles mixed with shrimp, onion, scallion, chili paste, and lime juice—half order)
- Yum gai (chicken salad with onion, lime juice, and chilies)

Note: Limit fish and chicken portions to four ounces and noodles to a half cup (picture five CDs stacked on top of each other).

STEER CLEAR OF THESE

- Tod man plaa (deep-fried fish cake with cucumber)
- Por pia tod (fried spring rolls)
- "Pad" (sautéed) dishes that contain a lot of oil
- Neua panang (red curry beef—beef slices sautéed in red curry, coconut milk, lemon leaves, sweet basil, and chili peppers)

Note: Prawns (goong) and other shellfish contain cholesterol; however, they contain very little saturated fat—the bigger culprit when it comes to elevating cholesterol levels.

Party-Time Tips

As a busy 30-something, you are no doubt attending parties on a regular basis: birthday celebrations, cocktail parties, charity events—you name it. No matter what occasion is next on your list, you can stay on your plan and still have fun. Here are my party-time tips.

- **Have a small snack before you go.** Pick a fruit-and-nut combo from your "A" snack list or a snack from your "B" list. Snacking before socializing can curb your hunger and will make you less likely to overindulge later on. It will also allow you to make better decisions about what to eat.
- **Wear your favorite outfit.** Choose something that you feel fabulous in—a fitted sweater with a slimming pair of jeans; a Tahari top with a leather skirt. You'll be less prone to overeat

if you are wearing something you love and feel fantastic in. A great pair of jeans with a belt can meet the criteria too.

- **Mingle one-on-one at cocktail hour.** The fewer people around you, the less you figure to eat, according to a study from Georgia State University. Specifically, a meal eaten with one other person tends to be 33 percent larger than a meal eaten alone. With two others, it is 47 percent larger, and with three, it climbs to 58 percent larger.
- **Watch the nuts and cheese.** Nuts, including almonds, walnuts, cashews, and macadamia nuts, are heart healthy but can contain up to 400 calories per half cup! Cheese is caloric as well. Brie and Swiss have about 100 calories per ounce. Mozzarella is a bit lower in calories—about 80 per ounce.
- **Make only one trip to the buffet.** Fill your plate *once*. And scan the entire spread before deciding what to eat. This can result in huge calorie savings. For instance, you may find that the fried chicken fingers become less of a draw when you spot the grilled shrimp farther down the line. If that's the case, better to be picky and spend your calories on foods that appeal to you the most.
- **Fill half your plate with salads and vegetable dishes.** Because, in general, you'll be consuming more calories at parties than you do at home, I recommend an altered party plate: half vegetables (or salads with low-fat dressings). Round out the rest of the plate with small portions of protein and grains.
- **Wait 20 minutes before finishing your last bites.** It takes 20 minutes for your stomach to tell your brain it's had enough food, so pausing for this amount of time before finishing your plate (or running for seconds) can help you control how many calories you consume.
- **Alternate alcoholic beverages with seltzer, diet soda, or water.** Rotating liquids will keep you hydrated and will help you cut calories from both alcohol and food, because you tend to eat more when you drink. (See sidebar entitled "Alcohol Guidelines.")

Alcohol Guidelines

On The 30s Health Prescription you can substitute one drink for your "C" snack. Or, you can do some extra cardio to offset the alcohol calories you consume. Either way, limit yourself to three drinks per week on the plan. Have your drink as close to a meal as possible because alcohol is absorbed faster without food in your system. Take a look at these calorie counts of some alcoholic beverages and their exercise equivalents:

DRINK	CALORIES	EXERCISE NEEDED TO BURN OFF
Kir Royale (2.5 oz)	75	17-minute brisk walk (4 mph)
Vodka or rum, 80 proof (1.5 oz)	96	22-minute brisk walk (4 mph)
White wine (5 oz)	100	13-minute jog
Red wine (5 oz)	106	14-minute jog
Beer (12 oz)	140	31 minutes of yoga
Cosmopolitan (5 oz)	264	26 minutes on the elliptical machine
White Russian (4 oz)	293	44 minutes of aerobics
Chocolate martini (5 oz)	376	67 minutes on the stationary bike

Note: Exercise equivalents are based on a 150-pound woman.

Source: ESHA database, www.drinksmixer.com

Dates (and Other Important Meetings)

For a date, business lunch, or any other important meeting, my number one piece of advice is to *never arrive hungry*. Having a snack before a date will keep your blood sugar stable after a long day of work or endless errands and will prevent you from feeling so ravenous that you can't hear a word your companion is saying. Eating beforehand also allows you to be in control of at least one part of the date—your hunger level.

As I've learned firsthand, you can't assume you're going to satisfy even mild hunger pangs on a date! Sometimes you may think you're going to end up having dinner, but the date seems to go on and on and on—without any indication that he's ready to ask if you'd like something to eat. If this happens, you will be that much better off for having had your snack. Having food in your system takes on even more importance if you're planning to have a drink, because alcohol is absorbed more quickly on an empty stomach, rendering you tipsier than you'd anticipated.

What should you eat before your date? Either an "A" or "B" snack, or even one of the dinner options. Each of these will tide you over in case you're not meeting for a meal. If you have already eaten and then wind up with a menu in your hands, order an appetizer—either a salad or a protein-rich dish. If you know ahead of time that you have a dinner reservation, follow the tips outlined earlier in the chapter.

Holiday Surprise

Believe it or not, the holiday season may *not* be the most fattening time of year. One recent study found that we gain only about one pound on average during the period between Thanksgiving and New Year's. The hitch is that we don't seem to lose that pound during the following spring and summer months, according to the study. So, over the years, the pounds add up! To avoid "the gift that keeps on giving," as Al Roker put it to me on "Today," be sure to exercise as often as possible during this time.

Vacations

Traveling can wreak havoc on your diet—whether you're eating in the airport, on the train, or in the car. One of the surest ways to come home without extra baggage is to pack your snacks. "A" snacks, especially the dried-fruit-and-nut combos, provide protein, fat, and fiber, to keep you satisfied during long trips and even during your stay when mealtimes are far apart.

Purchase Ziploc bags or containers, and measure out your portions in advance. Also, don't forget about exercise during your trip. If you're driving, stop and take a short walk; if you're on a plane, get up and walk the aisles. And once you're at your destination, try to do some brisk walking, and take advantage of any workout facilities in hotels. Being active can make the difference between gaining weight and not gaining weight during your vacation. Watch alcoholic beverages too—not only are they high in calories (an eight-ounce piña colada has more than 400!), but also they can contribute to dehydration and jet lag during air travel. Drink plain water as often as possible, and aim for eight ounces for every hour of flight to stay hydrated and minimize jet lag.

Maintaining a Healthy Lifestyle

11

Congratulations on your progress toward becoming a healthier, new you. You've made the investment, and, as with the various women profiled throughout this book, you stand to reap the well-deserved benefits, both physical and psychological. I picture you with new clothes, possibly a new relationship, and other opportunities and interests occupying your life that weren't there before.

So, how do you make sure the rewards of all of your efforts stay with you for the long term? Basically, you continue to follow the plan, with a few calorie tweaks. Remember, The 30s Health Prescription is a lifestyle. It's not a fad diet or other restrictive plan without staying power.

The 30s Health Prescription for Weight Maintenance

If, by consuming 500 fewer calories each day, you lost a pound each week and reached your target weight, it might seem logical to add back 500 calories to your diet, to keep your-self at your current weight. Unfortunately, real life doesn't work that way. The reason is that once you reach a lower body weight, your metabolism—or total calories burned—decreases. (I talked about this in Chapter 2.) Therefore, you need *fewer calories than before* to keep your body functioning at your new weight. Adding 500 calories back at this time could result in weight gain.

Let's take Erica as an example of this principle. When I first met Erica, she was consuming about 2,000 calories a day. This was the amount that was keeping her at her then-current weight. During our first session, I suggested that she follow the 1,600-calorie plan and include 30 minutes of exercise each day, so that she would reach a 500-calorie deficit to lose one pound each week (400 fewer food calories plus about 100 calories burned from her cardio workouts). Erica has since dropped 20 pounds on The 30s Health Pre-scription. But based on her current, smaller body weight, 1,600 calories is now her maintenance level. In fact, if Erica hadn't reached her weight goal yet and wanted to continue losing, she would have to consume even fewer calories, say 1,400 or so.

Once you reach your weight-loss goal, wait a few weeks or even months until you've stabilized. Continue following the plan, until your body gets accustomed to its new supply of energy. You may find that a few weeks or months later, you can start to gradually increase your calories while still main-taining your current weight. Remember to go slowly. Instead of increasing your portions, I recommend adding an extra "A" and "B" snack (of course, "C" snacks count too). You may find, however, that your calorie prescription for weight loss is now your maintenance level, as in Erica's case. If that's the case, you can just continue to follow your original plan in the days ahead.

Maintaining a Healthy Weight: Slimming Secrets

In addition to following the guidelines I've just laid out, here I'm going to share with you a few secrets that have helped many women maintain their fabulous new figures.

Keep a Journal

Writing down what you eat and how you feel about your food decisions is one of the best strategies to help maintain your weight, especially during nights out, holidays, trips, and other times when your eating environment is not the usual. It keeps you conscious of every bite that goes into your mouth, helping you to avoid mindless nibbling.

As relayed in Chapter 5, research has documented how effective keeping a journal can be, especially during high-risk times. Dieters who kept careful food records continued to lose weight during the holiday season, whereas those who didn't put back on some of the pounds they lost.

Never Skip Breakfast

Maintaining your weight involves eating breakfast daily. That's according to more than 5,000 successful "losers" from the National Weight Control Registry, which tracks women (and men) who have lost at least 30 pounds and have maintained the status for at least one year. True, skipping breakfast cuts calories in the short term, but your blood sugar, already low from an overnight fast, drops further by midmorning, making you ravenous and craving "C" snacks. This translates to more calories consumed later in the day—something I've seen time and time again among my 30-something clients. Skipping breakfast also causes your body to hold on to any conserved energy, instead of burning it. This slowdown in metabolism makes it harder to maintain your weight.

On top of metabolism benefits, eating breakfast gets your body up to speed in the morning, both physically and mentally. Plus, a breakfast on The 30s Health Prescription offers many nutrients specific to your needs, including those bone-building and antiaging nutrients.

If you don't have time for breakfast during your morning routine, or if you don't have the appetite for food first thing in the morning, take something small with you if you're on the go, so that when you're hungry, you'll be prepared. Many breakfasts on the plan are easily transportable, so you can fuel up wherever you may be.

Keep Moving

There's no doubt about it: if you're physically active, you're more likely to keep the pounds off. And for women like us, exercise is indispensable because we don't want to suffer the weight gain associated with a slowed metabolism. If the thought of heading to the gym seems like too much after a long day of work (for me, that's often the case), pick activities that will better suit your lifestyle.

I love brisk walking. In New York City, I can walk to my office, to the supermarket, to Saks, wherever. And with every 30 minutes of walking, I burn more than 100 calories.

I also enjoy meditative exercise such as yoga, which is relaxing and active at the same time. Plus, my new favorite is jazz-funk classes. I love to dance, but it's something I hadn't made time for. Now I look forward to it every Sunday morning.

Think Positive—Even If You Slip

Slipping off of the plan is OK; it's a reality of life. One of the major saboteurs to your diet is to think of a slip as a fall. The reason is you're likely to do more damage on future food occasions when you judge your eating behaviors too harshly.

The way you interpret your experiences greatly determines your future actions. In fact, I have encouraged all of the women you've read about in previous chapters to go easy on themselves if they ate something they felt they shouldn't have. If it happens that one day you ate too much pasta; another day too many "C" snacks—don't sweat it. It's OK. Really. Just get back on track the next day.

Avoid Triggers

Despite your strong willpower, it can be hard to resist tempting foods, desserts, whatever—when they're staring you in the face. There's much to be said for "out of sight, out of mind."

Do yourself a favor: make it easier to stick to your goals by avoiding your triggers. This could mean steering clear of the cookies at the supermarket, walking home on the path that doesn't pass your favorite pizza joint or ice cream shop, or avoiding restaurants where you are tempted to overdo it.

Be a Picky Eater

Always ask yourself: Do I *really* want this? Can I live without this now? Is there something else I would prefer to have, maybe later?

Amanda became a pro at being picky. Each time she was about to reach for a "C" snack or a drink, she stopped herself, to check in with her feelings. There were times when she skipped a dessert at a business lunch, thinking about the drink she would have with friends after work. Other times, she would have a drink at dinner but skip her "C" snack. As I explained to Amanda, it comes down to negotiating with yourself. Anything good is worth the effort, and the effort here comes from deciding what it is you really want.

Remember these three words: Stop; Think; Eat. When you've finished a meal but feel like having more, wait 20 minutes—the amount of time your stomach needs to tell your brain it's full. Embrace the delayed effect; you may find you can live without the extra food and calories. If you're still hungry after 20 minutes, it may be time to go for an "A" or "B" snack.

Don't Skip the Salad!

Eating a salad is one of the few occasions when *adding* an appetizer keeps you slim. That's what the research shows. As the main part of the meal, salads offer a great way to get your vegetables in without fussing too much.

Salads boost your fiber, vitamin, and phytochemical intake while keeping your calories in check during your meal. Eating them will help you keep the pounds off, as long as you don't overdo it with dressing, nuts, or fried meats. These high-cal extras can make a salad look more like a burger and fries, in terms of calories and fat.

Check In with the Scale Once Each Week

As I mentioned earlier, there's no need to weigh yourself every day. That habit can trip you up by revealing false highs or lows. Still, I recommend checking in with the scale on a weekly basis. By weighing yourself weekly, you'll be more likely to keep the pounds off, because you'll catch any real gains before you've done too much damage.

Wendy, a longtime client of mine, found that her weight often fluctuated a few pounds here and there, during and after her initial weight loss. We decided to define a limit for a gain, above which would be unacceptable and a red flag to change her eating habits. Wendy said that a five-pound gain on the scale, at any point in her life, would mean it's time to closely examine her eating and exercise habits (five pounds would be more than the two- to three-pound gain during her period and would represent true weight gain). It's worked well for Wendy so far; the scale has kept her weight in check and has kept her eating under control.

Have a Plan for Special Occasions

Whether it's going to a friend's party, out to a special dinner, or somewhere else where lots of food is ready and waiting, don't leave home without a plan. Whether your idea of planning means exercising earlier in the day; eating a light lunch, skipping your "C" snack, or all of the above, preparing yourself will make it easier for you to stay slim. Plus, the more you practice your healthful behaviors in high-risk situations, the easier it will become.

To make special occasions easier to manage, you may want to pick five or six days of the year on which you tell yourself it's OK to overindulge. It could be your birthday, your anniversary, Thanksgiving, Christmas/Hanukkah, New Year's, or another special day you celebrate. By selecting these days ahead of time, you free yourself of any guilt, which, in turn, will probably make it *easier* for you to avoid overdoing it. For more party-time tips see Chapter 10.

Buy New Clothes but Hold On to Old Pictures

When it comes to keeping the weight off, there's nothing more motivating than investing in a stylish new wardrobe. Once the slimming jeans fit, you won't want to push them to the back of the closet. You may want to post old pictures of yourself in a private place, to remind yourself how you looked before.

Continue to Find Meaning in What You're Doing

Last but certainly not least, never lose sight of *why* you're investing in yourself. I tell this to clients and friends all the time—figure out *why* being healthy and slim is important to you. It could be one goal or many; it could be living a long life or going on the hiking trip you've always dreamed of. Keeping a goal in the front of your head will make it that much easier to turn away from guilty pleasures when the temptation arises.

Now that you've learned the principles of The 30s Health Prescription, you have the tools you need to succeed at maintaining good health. I'm talking about a slim figure, beautiful hair, glowing skin, and lifelong vitality. With the sea of scientific information that surrounds us, it's easy to get lost. By using The 30s Health Prescription you will always be able to find your way. And remember—now is the time to feel strong, slim, and sexy—that is, now and *always*!

Food Substitution List

The food servings presented here can be used for making substitutions in your meal plan. To make a substitution, find the appropriate food group, then select the food you wish to substitute. Pay attention to the listed portion sizes, which differ for different items. For example:

- If your plan calls for ½ cup of pasta, you would substitute only ⅓ cup of rice because both are equal to one grain serving.
- If your plan calls for ¾ cup of fresh blueberries, you would substitute 1¼ cups of sliced strawberries because both are equal to one fruit serving.

Note: The nutrient criteria for each food group are adapted from the exchange lists for weight management by the American Dietetic Association and American Diabetes Association.

Fruit

Each fruit serving contains approximately 60 to 80 calories and 15 grams of carbohydrate.

Apple, medium: 1
Banana: ½ large or 1 extra small
Blackberries: 1 cup
Blueberries: ¾ cup
Cantaloupe: ⅓ medium or 1 cup cubes
Cherries: ⅔ cup
Cranberries, dried: 2 tablespoons
Cranberries, fresh: 1¼ cups
Dried apple rings: 4
Dried apricot halves: 8
Figs, medium: 2
Grapefruit, medium: ½
Grapes (red or green): 15
Honeydew: 1 small slice or 1 cup cubes
Mango, slices: ½ cup
Mixed fresh fruit: ½ cup
Nectarine, medium: 1
Orange, medium: 1
Peach, medium: 1
Pear, small: 1
Pineapple, slices: 2
Plum, small: 2
Raisins: 2 tablespoons
Raspberries: 1 cup
Strawberries, sliced: 1¼ cups
Tangerine, small: 2
Watermelon: 1 small slice or 1⅓ cups cubes

Vegetables

Each vegetable serving contains approximately 25 calories and 5 grams of carbohydrate. One serving is equal to ½ cup cooked or 1 cup raw vegetables.

Artichoke hearts
Asparagus
Beets
Broccoli
Brussels sprouts
Cabbage
Carrots (whole, shredded, and baby)
Cauliflower
Cherry tomatoes
Cucumber
Eggplant
Mixed vegetables, steamed
Mushrooms
Peppers
Salad greens (spinach, romaine, endive, arugula)
Snap peas
Spinach
Sprouts
Squash
Water chestnuts
Zucchini

Grains and Starches

Each grain serving contains approximately 80 to 100 calories and 15 grams of carbohydrate.

Bagel (4 ounces): ¼
Baked chips: 10

Baked potato with skin: ½
Beans, cooked: ⅓ cup
Bread, reduced-calorie: 2 slices
Bread, regular: 1 slice
Cereal, ready-to-eat: ¾ cup
Corn: ½ cup
Couscous, cooked: ½ cup
Croutons: 15
English muffin: ½
Granola: ¼ cup
Hummus: ¼ cup
Lentils, cooked: ⅓ cup
Matzoh: 1 sheet
Melba toast: 4 pieces
Muffin, low-fat (2 ounces): ½
Oatmeal, cooked: ½ cup
Pasta, cooked: ½ cup
Peas, green, cooked: ⅔ cup
Pita, 6½-inch: ½
Plantain: ½ cup
Popcorn, low-fat, microwave: 3 cups
Pretzels, tiny twists: 15
Rice, cooked: ⅓ cup
Rice cakes, mini: 10
Roll, small: 1
Saltines: 6
Sandwich bun: ½
Squash (butternut, acorn, pumpkin): 1 cup
Sweet potato/yam: ½ cup
Taco shell, low-fat: 1
Tortilla, 6-inch: 1
Waffle, low-fat, 4-inch: 1
Wheat Thins: 10

Low-Fat Dairy

Each low-fat dairy serving contains 80 to 100 calories and approximately 25 percent of the daily value for calcium.

Cheese, fat-free or low-fat: 2 ounces (note: calcium content of cheese varies)
Milk, fat-free or 1%: 1 cup
Yogurt, fat-free or low-fat: 6–8 ounces

Very Lean Protein

Each very lean protein serving contains approximately 30 to 45 calories, 6 to 7 grams of protein, and 1 gram of fat.

Cheese, fat-free: 1 ounce
Chicken breast (no skin): 1 ounce
Cornish hen (no skin): 1 ounce
Cottage cheese, low-fat or nonfat: ¼ cup
Duck breast (no skin): 1 ounce
Egg substitutes: ¼ cup
Egg whites: 2
Fish fillet (cod, flounder, halibut, trout, lox): 1 ounce
Lunchmeats, deli-sliced (chicken and turkey breast, ham, roast beef): 1 ounce
Shellfish (shrimp, scallops, lobster, crab, clams): 1 ounce
Tuna: 1 ounce
Turkey breast (no skin): 1 ounce

Lean Protein

Each lean protein serving contains approximately 50 to 70 calories, 6 to 8 grams of protein, and 3 grams of fat.

Beef, lean, trimmed of fat, select or choice (flank steak, round, sirloin, tenderloin): 1 ounce
Cheese, low-fat (3 grams of fat or less per ounce): 1 ounce
Chicken, dark meat without skin: 1 ounce
Cottage cheese (4% fat): ¼ cup
Herring: 1 ounce
Oysters: 8
Pork chop, lean: 1 ounce
Salmon: 1 ounce
Turkey, dark meat without skin: 1 ounce
Veal, lean, roast or chop: 1 ounce

Fats

Each fat serving contains approximately 40 to 55 calories and about 5 grams of fat.

Avocado: 3 tablespoons
Butter, hard: 1 teaspoon
Butter, whipped: 2 teaspoons
Cream cheese, regular: 1 tablespoon
Cream cheese, low-fat: 1½ tablespoons
Margarine, hard, stick: 1 teaspoon
Margarine, soft: 1½ teaspoons
Mayonnaise, regular: 1 teaspoon
Mayonnaise, light: 1 tablespoon
Nuts: 1 tablespoon
Oil (olive, canola, corn, vegetable): 1 teaspoon
Olives, black, large: 8
Olives, stuffed green, large: 10
Peanut butter or other nut butters: ½ tablespoon
Salad dressing, regular: 1 tablespoon
Salad dressing, low-fat: 2 tablespoons
Seeds (pumpkin, sunflower, sesame): 1 tablespoon

Sour cream, regular: 1½ tablespoons
Sour cream, reduced-fat: 2 tablespoons

Sweets ("C" Snacks)

Each serving of sweets contains approximately 100 calories.

Angel food cake: 1 piece (1½ ounces)
Animal crackers: 18
Brownie, fat-free, 2-inch square: 1
Candy bar, mini, Nestle Crunch; Kit Kat: 2
Chocolate pudding, fat-free: 1 cup
Cookie, chocolate chip, 2¼-inch: 1
Cupcake, with cream filling and frosting: ½
Frozen yogurt, low-fat: ½ cup
Fudge bar, fat-free: 1
Hershey's Kisses: 4
Honey: 1½ tablespoons
Ice cream, low-fat: ½ cup
Jam: 2 tablespoons
Jelly beans, small: 25
Licorice: 3 pieces
Mallomars: 2
M&Ms, Peanut: 10
Marshmallows, mini bag: 1
Nabisco 100-calorie pack: 1
Rice Krispies Treat: 1
Snackwell's bite-size chocolate chip cookies: 10
Snackwell's cookies (creme sandwich, devil's food cakes): 2
Sorbet: ½ cup
Syrup, chocolate: 2 tablespoons
Syrup, maple: 2 tablespoons
Tootsie Roll Midgees: 4

Calories Burned from Physical Activity

This chart shows the calories burned from various physical activities. The calorie counts are based on two different weights: 125 pounds and 150 pounds. The duration for each activity is 30 minutes.

ACTIVITY	CALORIES BURNED (125 LBS)	CALORIES BURNED (150 LBS)
Walking during work (office)	85	102
Dancing (ballet, jazz, tap)	135	163
Scrubbing the bathtub	107	129
Carrying groceries upstairs	212	254
Playing with children	113	136
Vacation involving walking	56	68
Stretching, hatha yoga	71	85
Sex (vigorous effort)	42	51
Cleaning the house	85	102
Vacuuming	99	119
Pushing child in stroller	71	85
Tai chi	113	136

Data from Ainsworth, B. E., The Compendium of Physical Activities Tracking Guide (http://prevention.sph.sc.edu/tools/compendium.htm), Univeresity of South Carolina Prevention Research Center, Arnold School of Public Health, University of South Carolina, January 2002.

Visualizing Portions on the Plan

Use the visual guides below to eyeball portion sizes:

FOOD	PORTION SIZE
1 cup of berries or vegetables	Medium-size fist
1 piece of fruit (apple, orange)	Baseball
½ cup of pasta or cereal	½ baseball
⅓ cup of rice	Cupcake wrapper
1 ounce of pretzels	Tennis ball
1 slice of bread	CD case
1 ounce of chicken, turkey, or meat	Matchbook
3 ounces of chicken or fish (tuna or salmon steak)	Deck of cards or computer mouse
3 ounces of fleshy whitefish (flounder or sole)	Checkbook
1 ounce of sliced cheese or luncheon meat	CD
1 ounce of hard cheese	4 dice
½ cup of ice cream or frozen yogurt	½ baseball
¼ cup of nuts, dried fruit, or granola	Golf ball
2 tablespoons of reduced-fat salad dressing	Ping-Pong ball or shot glass
1 teaspoon of olive oil or dressing	Standard cap on a 16-ounce water bottle
1 teaspoon of butter or margarine	Postage stamp

Adapted from Lisa R. Young, The Portion Teller, *New York: Morgan Road Books, 2005. Reprinted by permission.*

Index

SWEAT YOUR WORKOUT, NOT GETTING INTO YOUR JEANS.

WOMEN'S HEALTH WORKOUTS, NOW ON DVD.

Our fitness editors have put together the very best routines to help you shape your ideal body, no matter what your fitness goals. **Train for Your Body Type** helps you maximize your workouts based on your natural shape to achieve big results. And for that big day, **The Wedding Workout** is designed to help you look your best. Plus, it makes a great way to get in shape for any occasion.

Available wherever fitness DVDs are sold! To order, call (800) 266-9719 or visit womenshealthdvds.com.

IT'S GOOD TO BE YOU™

200734-002